I0213322

Journey
ON
Angel
Wings

Journey
ON
Angel
Wings

MY JOURNEY TO THE TRUTH

SHE WENT TO HEAVEN AND
WINGS APPEARED ON MY HOUSE

ALEX O'NEAL HEATON JR.

Halo
PUBLISHING
INTERNATIONAL

Copyright © 2024 Alex O'Neal Heaton Jr. All rights reserved.

No part of this publication may be reproduced, stored in a retrieval system or transmitted in any form or by any means, electronic, mechanical, photocopying, recording or otherwise, without prior permission of Halo Publishing International.

The views and opinions expressed in this book are those of the author and do not necessarily reflect the official policy or position of Halo Publishing International. Any content provided by our authors are of their opinion and are not intended to malign any religion, ethnic group, club, organization, company, individual or anyone or anything.

For permission requests, write to the publisher, addressed "Attention: Permissions Coordinator," at the address below.

Halo
PUBLISHING
INTERNATIONAL

Halo Publishing International
7550 W IH-10 #800, PMB 2069,
San Antonio, TX 78229

First Edition, November 2024
ISBN: 978-1-63765-671-6
Library of Congress Control Number: 2024918378

The information contained within this book is strictly for informational purposes. Unless otherwise indicated, all the names, characters, businesses, places, events and incidents in this book are either the product of the author's imagination or used in a fictitious manner. Any resemblance to actual persons, living or dead, or actual events is purely coincidental.

Halo Publishing International is a self-publishing company that publishes adult fiction and non-fiction, children's literature, self-help, spiritual, and faith-based books. We continually strive to help authors reach their publishing goals and provide many different services that help them do so. We do not publish books that are deemed to be politically, religiously, or socially disrespectful, or books that are sexually provocative, including erotica. Halo reserves the right to refuse publication of any manuscript if it is deemed not to be in line with our principles. Do you have a book idea you would like us to consider publishing? Please visit www.halopublishing.com for more information.

CONTENTS

INTRODUCTION

I'm not an author or a fan of writing, so this is going to be me, talking to you, with raw emotions and reactions. I want to make something clear up front. Due to my background and upbringing, many of the things I saw and discovered were not possible, in my mind.

I'm a retired US Army officer who met his wife while assigned to the 25th Light Infantry Division in Hawaii. What are the odds that a guy from Fayetteville, North Carolina, meets his wife from Paintsville, Kentucky, there?

Well, since this is the introduction, we were married for over thirty-eight years and had four kids and grandchildren. She went to heaven last year after she was unexpectedly diagnosed with stage 4 liver cancer. After the diagnosis, I took care of her in our house (home hospice), and it crushed me. If she could have stayed, I would have taken care of her forever, until the end of time, because that is how much I love her.

I love her more than anything. I still work for the Army (and have for about forty-two years) and was going to retire this year and travel with her around the world.

How much do I love her? At sixty years old, when I left work at the end of the day, I still get excited as I was walking across the parking lot to get in the car, knowing that I was going home to her. That's how much I love her.

After she transitioned, I cried all day and night; I thought about, and came close to, killing myself. The only things that kept me alive were the signs I received from her, and I have pictures of some, such as the angel wings that appeared on the side of our house and disappeared after a few minutes, an apostle-looking guy to the left of them; her face in a lighted candle; her face appearing in an orb on the floor next to our cat; a shaman showing up; and much more that is covered in the book.

I then did something that for my whole life, as a strong Catholic military officer, I thought was pure fake—I contacted a psychic medium. I wanted the best, so I contacted Catherine who had been tested and validated by a Harvard doctor. I pleaded with her to communicate with Julie. She agreed and brought evidence forward that she was communicating with my wife. I was shocked but still did not believe. She then told me I was a psychic medium also. I told her, no, I was not. So she said an owl would visit me at night, and I would be spiritually awoken. What nonsense, right?

I was in such disbelief I contacted a second psychic medium, Todd, who has worked for the New York City and Boston Police Departments on unsolved and missing-person cases. Well, Todd was able to communicate with my wife also, and then he said, "You don't need me, Alex; you're a psychic medium also. I can sense that." I told Todd, no, I was not and to stop saying that.

I'm still suicidal at this point, so a doctor recommended I try Ketamine IV infusion. I set up my first appointment and went. Ketamine IV infusion is like a legal near-death experience (NDE). I went through the tunnel, into the light, and saw the other side. I was frantically looking for Julie when angels grabbed me and took me to God.

I spoke with God for a while and told Him I wanted to see Julie; I missed her very much and was in pain. God said He understood. He feels all our pain and doesn't like it when we hurt each other. I was still focused on seeing Julie when God said, "Let Me let you feel how it feels to Me." I saw and felt the pain of the world for about thirty seconds (Ukraine and Russia, Israel and Hamas, etc.). God then told me to read the Book of Enoch, and He was adamant about that. I did not know who Enoch was at the time.

My oldest sister, Carol, is very religious; she took me to my first Ketamine IV treatment since I could not drive afterward. When I came back to this side—or world, if you prefer—I asked my sister who Enoch was and told her I had to read the Book of Enoch. Carol said, "Oh my God, I just ordered the Book of Enoch yesterday from Amazon." We were both shocked. I then asked my sister again who Enoch was; she told me he was the great-grandfather of Noah and was chosen by God to be taught by the archangels.

Still thinking about killing myself, I went back for a second Ketamine IV treatment and had the same near-death experience. The angels were waiting to take me to a pyramid in Egypt. The pyramid looked new, there were hieroglyphics, and I was inside. The angels asked me, "Now you understand?" I told them, no, I couldn't read that, but they told me that, yes, I could. After coming back to this world, I asked my sister about Enoch again and the pyramids. She said Enoch was thought to have built some of the pyramids to protect information from the Great Flood.

Next, Sanskrit words started showing up on the mirrors in my house. To see if I could connect with Julie, I also decided to start taking psychic-medium classes with a lady who is very renowned. I started praying and meditating a lot—something I never did before. My teacher told me I was very gifted, and right away, before I completed my training, which is very unusual, I started doing readings for people, both in person and with pictures from an online forum.

There's plenty more in this book. I hope it helps you to understand that God and heaven are real. *Our loved ones don't die; they transition and go to heaven. Before, I was probably 70-percent sure of this based on faith alone, but now I'm a 1,000-percent sure.* This book will make you feel love, sadness, joy, laughter, and certain that we are not separate from our loved ones who have transitioned.

CHAPTER 1

How It All Began: My Wife, Julie

I met my wife while serving in the Army, stationed with the 25th Light Infantry Division in Hawaii. It's incredible to think that a guy from Fayetteville, North Carolina, would cross paths with a girl from Paintsville, Kentucky, in such a distant place. Even now, as I write this, tears fill my eyes because of how deeply I love her. For most of my adult life, even as a teenager, I felt as if something was missing. But the moment I saw her, I knew she was the missing piece. This is just a glimpse of who Julie is—her kindness, compassion, and love.

Here's how we met: I was living in the US Army Schofield Barracks in Hawaii. One evening, my roommate, Ron, suggested we head out to Honolulu. I wasn't in the mood and told him no, but he kept insisting, so I finally gave in. It was a Tuesday, so I figured it wouldn't be as crowded as the weekends, so I reluctantly agreed to go.

Little did I know, Julie also didn't feel up to going out that night, but her friend convinced her to join anyway. As it turns out, neither of us wanted to go out that evening, but fate had other plans, and we ended up meeting.

I told Ron that we should find a quiet club in Honolulu, have a few drinks, and then head back. We ended up in a club with soft music playing in the background. I ordered a beer, while Ron, who didn't drink, got his usual Diet Coke. The place was nearly empty, so it didn't take long for me to spot Julie sitting with her friend. The moment we locked eyes, it felt as if I had known and loved her forever. I walked over, introduced myself, and as we started talking, it was as if I were in heaven with an angel. She was beautiful, kind, and soft-spoken. The love just radiated from us and has since that moment.

I could easily write another book about the incredible life I shared with Julie, but there's so much to cover, so I'll focus on a few key things that capture who she was on this earth. When I met Julie, she already had two daughters, Venus and Krystal, whom she loved deeply, both born in Hawaii. Julie's love extended to everyone and everything, including animals, insects, and plants. Her compassion was so powerful that I stopped hunting and fishing after meeting her, knowing how much she cherished all living creatures.

We got married on September 5, 1986, and not long after, we found out Julie was pregnant with our daughter, Maria. Julie was never one to want anyone fussing over her, so she often kept her pain or sickness to herself. You'd hardly know it if she was feeling unwell. She was a gentle, quiet person who didn't speak often, but when she did, people listened.

Marrying Julie was the best thing that ever happened to me. Everything I am, or will become, is because of her. Before meeting her, I was a young man without much direction. My parents were wonderful and loving, but as I mentioned earlier, something always felt missing until Julie came into my life.

Inspired by her, I started taking college classes in the evenings, determined to provide a better life for her. My career took off, and I quickly rose in rank, going from corporal to staff sergeant in just a few years. During this time, I also saved the life of another sergeant and was awarded an Army Commendation Medal for Lifesaving. At the ceremony, I asked if Julie could pin the medal on me, and my leadership agreed.

Shortly after Maria was born, I received orders assigning me to Vicenza, Italy, with the Southern European Task Force (SETAF). This was a blessing because my parents lived there, and they hadn't yet met Julie. My father, who retired from the US Army, had met my Italian mother when he was assigned to SETAF as a young man.

When we arrived in Italy, my parents instantly fell in love with Julie. How could they not? She was beautiful, kind, considerate, loving—truly an angel. Over time, my mother and father came to see Julie as their own daughter.

While stationed in Italy, I applied for the US Army Infantry Officer Candidate School (OCS) at Fort Benning, Georgia, and was thrilled when I got accepted. Julie never once complained about the frequent moves that come with Army life—she embraced it wholeheartedly. So we packed up and moved to Fort Benning, knowing that during OCS, I'd hardly get to see her.

After the first six weeks, we were finally allowed to call our wives. I called Julie, told her how much I loved and missed her, and mentioned how we were all starving from the intense physical activity. Julie, being the caring person she was, offered to sneak in some pizzas for me and the other guys. I knew it was against the rules, but we were so hungry at night that I agreed. Each night, I lowered my laundry bag down from the third-floor window with a rope, and Julie loaded it up with pizzas. The guys and I then sat quietly in the dark, enjoying those pizzas with big smiles on our faces, grateful for Julie's love and support.

One night, the guys in my platoon jokingly asked if Julie could sneak in some Dunkin' Donuts. Since sweets and soda were off-limits during OCS, it seemed like an impossible request. But I couldn't resist trying, so I snuck out to call Julie. Sure enough, that night she showed up with boxes of Dunkin' Donuts for all of us. It was a small act of kindness, but it meant the world to us.

I eventually graduated from Infantry Officer Candidate School and was commissioned as a second lieutenant in the US Army. I owe it all to Julie. Without her unwavering love and support, I don't think I would have made it to graduation.

As often happens in the military, a few years later, I received orders to return to Europe. While stationed at the base in Wiesbaden, Germany, Julie became pregnant but sadly had a miscarriage. It was a difficult time for us, but our love for each other helped us through it.

That year, Julie told me the day before Christmas that Maria, our daughter, had just mentioned wanting a Pippi Longstocking doll for Christmas. With heavy snow falling and the German stores about to close, I hesitated and asked Julie what I could do at that point. But when she looked at me with those beautiful eyes and a gentle tear rolling down her face, I knew there was no way I could say no.

Julie had this way of asking for something that I couldn't refuse. A tear in her eye was enough to break my heart, and she knew I'd walk through fire, take a bullet, or do whatever it took to keep her from being sad—that's how much I loved her. So I rushed out to the car, but, of course, it wouldn't start, and the snow was coming down hard. I ran back inside to tell Julie, and though she was disappointed, she said there was nothing we could do.

But I couldn't stand to see her sad, so I told her I'd put on my Army running clothes and run the ten miles downtown and back to get that doll. And that's exactly what I did. When I returned with the Pippi Longstocking doll, the happiness on Julie's face made every step worth it.

My next assignment took us to Fort McClellan, Alabama, where Julie became pregnant, and our son, Alex (Chip) Heaton III, was born. Julie, who grew up in the small town of Paintsville, Kentucky, nestled in the Appalachian foothills, found herself a bit uneasy with the role of being an Army officer's wife. The social expectations that came with being an officer's wife at that time were a bit outside of her comfort zone.

Shortly after we arrived at Fort McClellan, the general's wife organized a coffee gathering for all the officers' wives. Julie, being naturally quiet and shy around strangers, asked if she really had to go. I told her it was entirely up to her, but assured her she'd be fine if she decided to attend. In the end, she chose to go.

That evening, when I got home, I asked Julie how it went. To my surprise, she told me she had a great time. She had ended up sitting right next to the general's wife, sharing the same small sofa chair, and they struck up a conversation about making Southern fried chicken. Julie had found a new friend, and the general's wife ab-

solutely adored her for her down-to-earth, comforting personality.

After being assigned to an Army base in Virginia, from which I would eventually retire, Julie asked if she could adopt a dog from the Society for the Prevention of Cruelty to Animals (SPCA) shelter. I agreed, knowing that we now had a home with a fenced backyard, and understanding how much Julie loved animals. Julie mentioned that she would visit different SPCA shelters in the area and let me know when she found a dog she liked.

One day, while I was still on duty in the Army, she called me, excited, and asked if I could meet her at the SPCA shelter on my way home from work because she had found the dog she wanted. I left work in my Army uniform and headed to the shelter to meet her.

When I arrived, Julie was waiting for me in the parking lot, and we walked inside together. As we approached a cage, I hoped the dog she had chosen wasn't too big or one that yapped a lot.

To my surprise, inside the cage was a yellow male Lab missing a paw. Shocked, I said, "Julie, that dog is missing a paw." She calmly replied that she knew. I asked, "There are literally a hundred dogs in this shelter with all four paws. Why pick the one missing a paw?"

Julie looked at me and said, "Because I can take care of him and make him an artificial paw." The look in her eyes told me this was the dog she wanted, so we took him home. We named him Buddy, and he quickly became a beloved member of our family until he passed away. Yes, in case you're wondering, Buddy is in heaven with Julie.

A few years later, a similar situation arose—this time, Julie felt that Buddy, our Lab with the missing paw, needed a companion. She began searching through local SPCA shelters and eventually found a female yellow Lab. Just like before, she called me, and I left work, still in uniform, to meet her at the shelter.

When I arrived, Julie led me to a cage where a female yellow Lab lay; she was missing most of her fur due to malnutrition and a skin condition. I mentioned that there were other yellow Labs in the shelter that weren't missing their fur, but Julie, with her characteristic determination, assured me that she could nurse this one back to health. Seeing that familiar look in her eyes, I knew this was the dog she wanted. So we took her home and named her Buffy. She became a cherished part of our family until she, too, passed away. And, yes, Buffy is also in heaven with Julie.

During this time, our son, Chip, was getting old enough to play community baseball, so I decided to coach, having played the sport myself while growing up. Julie volunteered to be the team mom, and for the next five years, we worked side by side—me coaching and Julie supporting the team in every way she could.

Why is this important? In our community, some families couldn't afford the extra expenses for baseball gear like gloves, cleats, helmets, pants, and socks. Julie, always generous, volunteered to buy the necessary equipment for those children. With the parents' permission, she went to Dick's Sporting Goods and purchased everything the kids needed to be part of the team. Julie loved being the team mom and watching Chip play baseball. He was a talented left-handed pitcher.

It was also common for Julie to discover that some families in our community couldn't afford Christmas gifts for their children. As you might guess, she quietly bought and wrapped toys, delivering them to those families without seeking any recognition. Julie did all of this and more out of the kindness of her heart—because she truly cared about people.

Years later, when Buddy and Buffy passed away from different illnesses, Julie was there by their sides, comforting them in their final moments. Though heartbroken, she found solace in knowing they would be taken care of in heaven.

There are just two more brief stories I'd like to share with you to help you understand who Julie really was.

After retiring from the US Army as an active duty officer, I was hired back by the Army as a Department of the Army civilian. At this time, we lived in a very wooded area of Virginia, having moved to a bigger house.

One day, I came home to find a squirrel in our house. Naturally, I was surprised, but Julie explained that the squirrel had fallen from a tree and hurt her leg. She was determined to nurse the squirrel back to health before releasing her outside. I reminded her that squirrels aren't house pets and suggested letting it go immediately, but it was clear the squirrel was limping. Julie, being who she was, cared for the squirrel until it was healed; then she released it in our front yard, where there were plenty of trees, on a sunny day.

But that isn't the end of the story. One evening, I came home from work to find Julie standing in our front yard and making a clicking sound with her mouth. To my amazement, the squirrel she had nursed came running down from the top of a tree, climbed up her pant leg, and took a nut from her hand before scampering back up the tree. It was one of the craziest things I'd ever seen.

Julie's compassion didn't stop at squirrels. If there was a fly or moth in the house, she insisted it be captured alive and released back outside. If a bird's nest fell from a tree, my son, one of his friends, or I had to get a ladder and place the nest back in the tree, ensuring the baby birds or eggs were safe.

So it came as no surprise one evening when I found Julie feeding a stray momma cat. I told her not to feed the cat, warning that it would never leave, but Julie didn't listen. She even started hiding her feeding sessions from me.

One day, when I asked Chip if his mom was still feeding the stray, he just laughed and said, "Come on, Dad, you know Mom. She's feeding the stray momma cat, the squirrels, the rabbits, the deer, the raccoons, and of course the birds."

It finally dawned on me why our yard often looked like Noah's Ark. Eventually, the momma cat had kittens, and, soon enough, they moved into our house because, according to Julie, it was either too hot or too cold for them to stay outside all the time.

But that was Julie—a beautiful soul with an endless love for every living thing. I love her more than words can describe and always will.

CHAPTER 2
Diagnosis: Illness

J ulie was a small, energetic woman who always stayed active. Many days, I struggled to keep up with her while working in the yard. She loved being outside, whether it was tending to the garden, working on the flower beds, or simply enjoying nature. Along with her love for the outdoors, she had a soft spot for animals, often feeding everything that wandered near our home, including the neighbors' dogs and cats. I always wondered how the neighbors knew to come to our house when they lost their pets.

A year earlier, in 2022, a stray kitten had started coming to our house because, as usual, Julie was feeding him. My son and I quickly became attached to this kitten. He was friendly and made a beeping sound, which we found both cute and amusing. Julie, of course, loved him too.

But, one day, Beeps, as I named him, disappeared. We were all worried, and Julie searched everywhere— asking neighbors and checking with local animal shelters—but Beeps was nowhere to be found. As winter approached, with snow and ice on the ground, we continued to worry and search for him, but there was no sign of Beeps. We didn't know then, but Beeps would become important later.

In May 2023, Julie began to experience mild stomach pains. At first, she thought she had pulled a muscle while working in the yard. But by June, the pain hadn't gone away, so she decided to visit an express medical clinic. The doctor there assured her it was probably just a stomach bug and that it would pass in a few weeks. However, the pain persisted and even worsened.

During the first week of July 2023, brimming with excitement, Julie called me at work—Beeps had returned! She immediately took him to the vet for his shots and carried him back home, placing him in the room with me, knowing how much I cared for him. We were both overjoyed that Beeps had come back, though we couldn't understand how he had survived for a year, especially through the harsh winter. We even asked neighbors far and wide, but none had taken care of him. It was a mystery, but we were just happy to have him back.

By the second week of July 2023, Julie's pain got so bad that I took her to the emergency room at a major hospital. Despite the discomfort, Julie had remained active until that point. The emergency room doctors decided to run some tests and do scans. The results came back with devastating news: stage 4 liver cancer. The medical team, which included oncologists, informed me that there wasn't much they could do. It was hard to believe that, even in 2023, with all the advances in medicine, there was nothing that could be done for stage 4 cancer.

Julie made it clear she didn't want to stay in the hospital or go elsewhere for care. Instead, she chose home hospice, and I gladly agreed to take care of her because of how much I loved her. It was surprising to me, though, that there were no viable treatments available.

Reflecting on it now, it is uncanny that Beeps returned just a week before Julie was diagnosed with cancer, as if he somehow knew I was going to need his companionship.

As her condition worsened, Julie could no longer climb the stairs to our bedroom, so we set up a single bed in a downstairs room next to a full bathroom. The room was small, so I slept on the floor beside her bed, staying with her around the clock to care for her.

Many nights, I hardly slept. I spent hours watching her sleep or researching potential treatments on my laptop. A few times, I thought I had found something promising—for example, a drug being used in Israel, but it hadn't been approved for use in the US. I was also trying to get her into Johns Hopkins Hospital in Maryland, hoping for a miracle.

As with any cancer diagnosis, there were good days and bad days. Julie still didn't like being indoors, so I often helped her walk outside to sit in the fresh air. She never complained, but I could see the worry in her face—not for herself, but for me and the children. She didn't want me to tell the children what was wrong with her and asked me to keep it from them for as long as possible. Eventually, I had to gently let them know. Julie also insisted that I only ask the children to visit on her better days because she didn't want them to see her suffering and feel sad. Her love for me, our children, our grandchildren, and even the animals was boundless, and she always put others before herself.

As the weeks went by, it broke my heart to see her getting worse, but I remained positive in front of her. When Julie said things such as, "I know this is hard on you, honey," or "I'm sorry, honey; I love you so much," I reassured her saying, "Don't worry, honey. I'll figure something out to make you better."

One time, though, I couldn't hold it in any longer. I broke down in front of her, tears streaming down my face, and said, "Julie, I love you so much, honey."

She looked at me with such tenderness and replied, "I love you more than anything in the world."

I still don't know why I lost control in that moment, but it felt like a special, almost transcendent moment between us. As we told each other how much we loved each other, it was as if we had left this world and were somewhere peaceful and beautiful together.

As Julie grew closer to transitioning and going to heaven, she began seeing her mom and dad. She would tell me, "Daddy came to see me, and he looked really good." At night, I could hear her talking in her sleep, saying things such as, "I'm not ready yet, Mom."

Throughout this entire period, I prayed to Jesus and God every night, begging them to heal Julie. I pleaded with them to take me instead of her, or to let her stay so I could take care of her forever.

CHAPTER 3

She Goes to Heaven:
I'm Very Sad and Suicidal

Julie transitioned to heaven on August 24, 2023, the same day she was born. I was by her side, holding her in my arms as she transitioned, tears streaming down my face. During those final days, my friend Marcello, a former combat medic in Afghanistan, stayed with me. He was there for the last two nights of Julie's life, letting me know when the time was near. I am deeply grateful to him for being there for both of us.

As they gently took Julie from our home in the early hours of August 24, at 2:30 a.m., she looked so beautiful and peaceful. I went outside, into the darkness, looked up at the sky, and prayed to God, asking Him to please take care of Julie until I could join her. I never felt anger toward God because I knew He would reunite us one day, and I was thankful that He had brought this angel into my life.

The pain of losing her is unbearable. I know Julie wouldn't want me to be sad—she was a beautiful lady, with an equally beautiful soul, who loved people, animals, and nature. She had the heart of an angel, and I miss her so much. I have cried every day since her passing. To be clear, this Army soldier, the son of a retired Army soldier, was not one to cry often before this.

I knew Julie was now with her dad and mom, healthy and at peace, but I missed her terribly. My heart was broken. She was my love, my world. I kept thinking I couldn't live without her, but I knew I needed to stay strong for our children, at least long enough to witness her Celebration of Life services.

My daughter, Maria, and son, Chip, were extremely helpful in planning the services for their mother. I am also deeply grateful to my friend Mark, a retired US Army colonel, who supported me tremendously during this time. There were many other family members and friends who were there for us, and to all of you, I will be forever grateful: Kris (Maria's better half); Summer (Chip's better half); Venus (my stepdaughter) and her husband, Andrew, from Hawaii; Randy, Tina, Ruby, and Dena (dear friends); and, of course, my wonderful and loving older sisters, Carol and Linda.

Linda was able to come down right after Julie transitioned, but my oldest sister, Carol, was in Italy with our mother and father. My father had been dealing with heart issues over the past few months, and we weren't sure how serious they were. After learning about Julie's cancer, I asked my mom and sisters not to tell my dad, as I didn't want to add to his worries with his heart condition. Instead, we told him a small white lie—that I was having back pains again, which is why I couldn't get to Italy to see him. Being a 100-percent US Army disabled veteran, my dad knew I had back problems from my service, so he accepted the explanation.

My daughter, Maria, played a crucial role in ensuring that Julie's service and program were exactly as her mom would have wanted. Julie loved Stevie Nicks, so we chose her music for the Celebration of Life services. Many family members and friends attended the service, including Scott and Cody, friends of Chip, who were like sons to Julie and me.

There were also many active-duty and retired military members in their uniforms. I'm especially grateful to Lieutenant General (LTG) Gervais, the deputy commanding general of Training and Doctrine Command, and Mr. Formica, the executive deputy to the commanding general, for attending. Their presence meant so much to me and my family, and I'm sure Julie, who loved the Army and Army families, would have appreciated it deeply. During the service, Marcello joked, "I bet we won't have this many high-ranking military officers at our service when we transition." Julie was indeed very special and had a deep love for her country and the US Army.

Julie's service was held on August 30, 2023. On the morning of her service, I received a call from the car dealership; Julie's yellow Hummer H3 was finally ready to be picked up. Julie, despite being only five foot one, loved driving that yellow Hummer. It had been in the shop, waiting for a part, since June. I rushed over to the dealership before the service to pick it up and decided to drive it to her service, knowing she would have liked that.

The service was beautiful, but I found myself crying most of the time. I knew I needed to speak, so I gathered the strength to do so. I'm also deeply thankful to Pastor Art Wolz, who provided immense comfort to me and our family during this difficult time. When Pastor Art called me up to speak, I hadn't prepared anything because of my overwhelming grief. I wondered how I could possibly capture the essence of who Julie was in just a few words.

I decided to share with everyone that, besides her deep love for family and friends, Julie was the kind of person who brought Christmas to children who wouldn't have had one, bought baseball gear for kids whose families couldn't afford it, adopted a dog with a missing paw because she knew she could take care of him, and even brought a squirrel into our home to nurse it back to health after it injured its leg. That was Julie—a beautiful woman, with a beautiful soul, who did kind things for others quietly, without needing recognition. She truly was an angel.

The day after Julie's service, I decided to return to our house. I hadn't been staying there since the night she passed because of my overwhelming grief and the deep longing to join her on the other side. I have to thank Chip and Summer for letting me stay on their couch after Julie transitioned. They offered me a spare bedroom, but I didn't want to be alone, so I chose to sleep on their big L-shaped couch.

Many times, my son, Chip, slept on the couch beside me, offering comfort with his quiet presence. Summer cooked and tried to get me to eat, though I had little appetite. She has a calming effect on everyone around her and always listens with compassion. Reflecting on it now, it feels poignant—a US Army veteran finding solace in sleeping beside his son on a couch. It was comforting for me during that difficult time.

The day after the service, I returned to the house with my sister Linda, Chip, and Summer. After heading upstairs to take a shower and change clothes, I came back down to the living room and was immediately struck by the smell of burnt toast. I asked Linda and Summer, who were sitting in the living room, who had burned the toast. They both replied that they hadn't. Chip was outside in the front yard and hadn't been in the house. I insisted that I smelled burnt toast. Then, both Linda and Summer noticed the strong scent as well.

Julie had always liked to make her toast very crunchy, almost burnt, to eat with her oatmeal. The smell of burnt toast in the mornings was familiar to me—it was how I knew Julie was up and in the kitchen, making herself breakfast as I left for work. We were all surprised by the smell that filled the room. It was the first sign I received from Julie, letting me know she was still with me.

CHAPTER 4

Seeking Help: Unbelievable Signs

I'm in deep grief, and thoughts of suicide have crossed my mind more than once. I pray to God multiple times a day, asking for His help and guidance. In my search for help, I initially went down the conventional path, as it was all I knew. The idea of exploring anything outside of that—what I once considered unconventional methods—seemed like utter nonsense, even quackery. Looking back now, I realize just how wrong I was.

Given my background as a Catholic, a US Army chemical officer, and the recipient of an MBA in comptrollership, I never believed in things like ghosts, spirits, psychics, mediums, the power of crystals, tarot cards, or healing with hands. To me, all of that was just nonsense. Julie, on the other hand, was very spiritual and believed in some of those things. She had crystals and often picked up random stones from the ground because she could feel some sort of energy from them. I always told her not to bring those things into the house, thinking we shouldn't mess with such matters.

It was August 31, 2023, the day after Julie's services. My sister Linda was still in town and staying at a local hotel. I asked her to please meet me at my house so I could feed the cats, including Beeps. I left my son's house and met Linda at mine; she was already there when I arrived.

We both went inside, sat in the living room, and spent the day talking. I'm so grateful to Linda for being there for me. As the day went on, I had moments in which I broke down and cried, and other moments when I managed to hold it together. That evening, we planned to meet at Chip and Summer's house to get together with Venus and Andrew.

As I was getting ready to leave, around 8:30 p.m., I asked Linda if she would go with me to say goodbye to Julie, to let her know we were leaving and that I would be back. She agreed, so we walked down the long, dark hallway to the small bedroom where Julie had slept before she transitioned. As we approached the doorway, still in the dark hallway, I called out, "Julie, I love you, honey. We're going over to Chip's house." Then I said, "Julie, I love you. Julie, I love you. Julie, I love you so much."

Suddenly, what appeared to be a portal opened up in the bedroom. A man appeared first, looking confused, and then Julie appeared in a white dress, looking perfectly healthy but a little sad. She stood there for about a minute, just looking at me, and I was in complete disbelief. After Julie vanished, I turned to my sister and asked, "Linda, did you see what I just saw?"

She replied, "I saw Julie standing there in a white dress."

I said, "So it wasn't just me; we both saw it." We were both shocked, unable to believe what we had just witnessed.

As we prepared to leave my house, I turned to Linda and asked, "Should we tell Venus, Maria, and Chip what we just saw, or keep it to ourselves?"

She hesitated and replied, "I don't know."

I then suggested, "When we get to Chip's house, let's pull Andrew aside and ask him." Andrew, Venus's husband, is a great guy and very much connected to his Native Hawaiian roots. From my time stationed at an Army base in Hawaii, I knew that Native Hawaiians are very spiritual people, so I thought he might have some insight.

Hawaiian culture has a deep spiritual connection to the natural world and believes in the presence of spirits and ancestors. The concept of 'uhane as the spirit, soul, or animating force is significant in the Hawaiian culture. Hawaiians traditionally have a strong belief in the interconnectedness of the physical and spiritual realms, and they often acknowledge the presence of spirits and ancestors in their daily lives.

In Hawaiian spirituality, the veil between the living and the dead is seen as very thin, and it is believed that spiritual encounters are a natural part of life. Hawaiians may feel, see, hear, or sense the presence of spirits or ancestors in various forms, such as through dreams, visions, or signs in nature.

We arrived at Chip's house and went inside. The children were playing, and I saw Venus, Andrew, and Summer. Quietly, I approached Andrew and whispered, asking if I could speak with him outside for a moment. He nodded and followed me outside, where Linda was already standing in the yard. It was August, but the evening was comfortably cool and unusually quiet—no dogs barking, no children playing, and no sounds from passing cars.

Andrew asked in his native Hawaiian-English accent, "What's going on?"

I replied, "Andrew, something amazing happened. Linda and I saw Julie in the house as we were leaving."

He looked over at Linda, searching for confirmation, and saw the same look of shock and surprise on her face that I had on mine.

Linda simply said, "We saw Julie."

Andrew, not surprised at all, calmly explained that in Hawaiian culture, it's believed that such things are possible. He then shared that when his father transitioned, he would visit his mother at night when she first retired to lie down in bed, and both his mother and other family members had seen his father. I then asked Andrew if he thought we should tell Venus, Maria, and Chip. He said it was up to me, but he didn't see anything wrong with telling them.

I was concerned about how sharing this might affect their emotional state, but I decided to tell them anyway. At first, they seemed shocked, but when Linda confirmed the apparition, they seemed more accepting. Linda is a very logical, straight-shooter type of person, but also very kind.

It was September 1 when my sister Carol called from Italy to tell me that our father wasn't doing well. Before we discovered Julie's condition, I had been talking with my mom and Carol about my father's failing heart. Even after Julie received her diagnosis, she urged me to fly to Italy to see my father, assuring me that she would be okay while I was gone. But I couldn't bring myself to leave her side. She needed me, and I loved her too much to leave her at that time. Julie always put others before herself, and I knew that about her.

On September 2, Carol called again to tell me that our father had passed, just nine days after Julie left us. I was in shock. How could two people I love so much leave me so close together?

Then I had a moment of panic, wondering what my dad would think when he arrived in heaven and found Julie there, waiting for him with the rest of the family. He had no idea that Julie had been sick or that she had passed. But then I realized he would likely be comforted to see her—he loved her like a daughter. During this time, I was incredibly thankful that my oldest sister, Carol, was in Italy with our mom and dad. Thank you, Carol.

Around this time, in my desperation to hear from Julie, I started using an electronic voice phenomenon (EVP) program. Naturally, I was skeptical, as I've always been about mediums and anything related to the psychic realm. But I was desperate, so I thought I'd give it a try.

In the fields of ghost hunting and parapsychology, electronic voice phenomenon (EVP) refers to sounds, captured on electronic recordings, that are believed to be the voices of spirits or ghosts. Parapsychologist Konstantīns Raudive, who brought attention to the concept in the 1970s, characterized EVP as typically brief, often the length of a single word or a short phrase.

Julie was very close to my father and mother. They often told both of us that they considered her their own daughter. But Julie was wonderful, so I knew, even before they met her, that they would love her. After everything that happened, I started using an EVP program on my cell phone, monitoring it closely. Then, on September 2, 2023, I saw the words "AL TOGETHER" appear on the screen. My father's name was Alex, but everyone called him Al. I was stunned—was I reading this right? Was Julie telling me that she and my father were together on the other side? I took a screenshot and sent it to my sisters, who also believed it was Julie letting me know that she and my father were together.

Even with this sign, I found it hard to fully believe. But as time passed, I started receiving more messages, similar to this one, through the EVP program, and it became harder to dismiss them as mere coincidences.

My father was a great man, and I love and miss him dearly. He served for twenty-six years in the Army and did two tours in Vietnam. As a boy, I remember worrying about him every single day he was in Vietnam. My father was not only a great dad, but also a best friend to me. When I was stationed at an Army base in Italy, my parents lived just ten minutes away from Julie and me.

We often visited their house to eat or go out to dinner together. My dad and I would start drinking red wine and joking around, trying to make each other laugh more. My mom would often tell us, "You two need to be quiet and stop laughing so much when you're drinking." Julie would sit there, quietly smiling as she watched us.

I'm not sure if I ever fully grieved after my father's passing because I was already in so much grief over losing Julie. Every day, I found myself thinking about joining her. The pain I felt was indescribable—as if knives were stabbing my chest—and I had a constant knot in my throat. I was also losing weight from not eating. Knowing I needed help, I reached out to a couple of therapists.

The first person I contacted was a wonderful lady named Ashley, who specialized in trauma and PTSD counseling. Ashley also practiced something called EMDR—eye movement desensitization and reprocessing. EMDR is a type of trauma-focused cognitive behavioral therapy designed to reduce the intensity of traumatic memories. As you progress, it helps your brain reprocess these memories, making them less painful. I was experiencing a lot of pain and grief from the memory of seeing my beautiful wife pass, so I decided to try EMDR.

When I first spoke to Ashley, we clicked right away on the phone, and I felt very comfortable talking to her. She set up a time for us to meet on September 5, and that's when she began helping me with EMDR therapy.

During our first session, I could barely speak because I was overwhelmed with emotion, crying as I tried to explain how much pain I felt from Julie's passing. I told her how much I loved Julie and how traumatic it was for me to witness her transition to heaven at 2:30 a.m. on August 24. I couldn't get that image out of my mind, and I often thought about wanting to leave this world to join Julie. I also told her that I had been waking up, wide-awake, at 2:30 a.m. every morning since, unable to fall back asleep.

Ashley assured me, "I can help you with that." Then, at my second appointment with Ashley, I went in and we sat down in her very relaxing, large office furnished with couches and chairs. As I settled onto the couch, she looked at me and said, "Alex, I need your help."

I was puzzled by her request but responded, "Okay, how can I help you?"

She then explained that ever since our first session, she had been waking up at 2:30 in the morning, wide-awake, and unable to fall back asleep. She mentioned that she had children in school and needed her rest to take care of them. With a somewhat-surprised smile, she asked if I could help her stop waking up at 2:30 a.m. every morning.

I told her I would pray and ask Julie if she could help as well. I had been talking to Julie every day since she transitioned, but up to that point, I hadn't received any clear responses.

At my next appointment with Ashley, I asked if she was still waking up at 2:30 a.m. every morning.

She told me she wasn't and said, "Whatever you did seemed to work."

Although Ashley was very helpful to me, I was still overwhelmed by my grief, still thinking about taking my own life, and missing Julie so much. In my desperation, I decided to try connecting with a psychic medium to see if they could reach Julie. I was skeptical, of course, thinking that such things weren't possible and that all psychic mediums were fake. But my desperation to hear from Julie pushed me to try.

I began researching on the internet to find a medium who seemed credible. That's when I came across a psychic medium named Catherine. What initially drew me to Catherine was her background as a math teacher—something that resonated with my logical side. I was also impressed that she had been tested and certified in three research experiments conducted by Gary Schwartz, PhD, at the University of Arizona, as detailed in his book *The Afterlife Experiments*. Dr. Schwartz, who earned his doctorate from Harvard University, had joined the psychology and psychiatry departments at Yale University before moving to the University of Arizona, where he was a professor of psychology, medicine, neurology, psychiatry, and surgery by 2023.

On September 11, 2023, I called Catherine and asked her to please contact Julie for me. I was crying as I explained what happened and desperately asked for help. At the time, I didn't know that Catherine was also a professional astrologer, which made sense given her background in math.

Catherine agreed to do a reading for me on September 14, but she mentioned that she had felt something unusual while we were talking. She then asked me to send her my date, time, and place of birth, which I did.

On the morning of September 14, Catherine called me and connected me with Julie. I was in tears and complete shock as she provided me with information that there was no way she could have known about Julie.

Then, Catherine told me that after the feelings she had during our conversation and after analyzing my astrological data, she believed that I was also a psychic medium and that I had a gift.

I was skeptical and said, "No, I don't think so."

She explained that my astrological chart, with aspects like a Scorpio moon and five water planets, was similar to those of well-known psychic mediums, like James Van Praagh. Despite her explanation, I still had trouble believing it.

Catherine then asked if I had seen ghosts or spirits as a child. I told her I didn't think so. She urged me to think again, and I recalled that up until I was about nine years old, I did see them. Catherine went on to tell me that she didn't often tell people they were psychic mediums—in fact, that occurred rarely, if ever. Sensing my continued doubt, she emphasized, "Alex, I don't say this to everyone," and added, "This is going to happen quickly for you." She asked if I meditated.

I laughed, saying, "No, that's not something we do in the Army."

She responded, "Well, if you want to hear from Julie, you need to meditate." She also told me that I would receive signs, possibly be visited by an owl, and experience a spiritual awakening. When I asked how that would happen, she suggested it might come in a dream. I told her that if it came in a dream, I wouldn't take it seriously and would just think it was my imagination. She calmly replied, "Okay, the other side will find another way."

Although some of this sounded pretty crazy to me, Catherine came across as a very bright and insightful person.

I should briefly mention the whole experience of seeing ghosts or spirits as a child. Up until I was about nine or ten years old, I did see spirits. Although I never felt as if they were there to harm me, they did scare me at that age. The spirits came into my room to visit me, and I still remember two of them vividly to this day—a beautiful lady with blonde hair in a white dress and an older man sitting in a rocking chair by my bed. Of course, when this happened, I would run to my mom and tell her, and she would walk into my room and say, "I don't see anything."

Up until I was about ten years old, I often left my bedroom at night and went to sleep either at the foot of the bed or on the floor in one of my sisters' rooms. For some reason, the ghosts or spirits didn't follow me into their rooms. My parents and sisters just assumed I was afraid of the dark, though I wasn't. You can imagine the good-natured teasing I got from my two older sisters when I joined the Army and was assigned to the elite 101st Airborne Division—especially since they thought I was afraid of the dark as a kid!

Taking Catherine's advice to heart, I started meditating in hopes of hearing from Julie. I meditated from the moment I woke up in the morning until late in the evening when I went to bed. Clearing my mind was incredibly difficult; normal thoughts kept racing through my head, such as needing to change the oil in my car, thinking about how I could join Julie, and reminding myself to get cat food. But I kept meditating and refused to give up. My daily routine became waking up, meditating, eating a small snack, meditating until dinner time, possibly eating dinner, and then meditating until I passed out.

One day, I decided to search the internet for guided meditations and came across one that helps you ask your loved ones who have passed to send a sign. I selected this meditation and listened closely as the guide walked me through the process. She mentioned that when you ask for a sign, you can't be too specific—for example, asking for a bluebird to sit on your porch at a particular time. The bluebird might show up somewhere else instead.

I followed the meditation closely, and with my eyes closed and listening to the soft music, I asked Julie to show me a yellow or orange butterfly. Julie loved butterflies. After meditating, I went outside, but it was pouring down rain and supposed to rain all day. I thought to my-self, *There's no way Julie can send me a butterfly in this weather.*

Later that same day, my son came by the house to take care of some flowers that were still in the garage from Julie's Celebration of Life service. I had told him I couldn't bring myself to do it and asked if he could come by one day to take care of it. He planted what he could and cleaned up the garage, all while it was still raining. About an hour later, he came inside, where I was sitting in the living room, and asked me to come outside to the front yard to see something. I initially refused, telling him it was raining and that I was feeling too sad. But he kept insisting, so I finally got up and went outside with him, still in the rain.

He led me over to one of Julie's gardens and showed me where he had placed a yellow-and-orange plastic butterfly in the garden. I started crying. It was a definite sign from Julie, a message of love to both me and Chip. I later shared the meditation with Chip, feeling deeply touched by this connection.

In the late afternoon of September 14, around 4:00 p.m., I was outside in my front yard, talking to my sister Linda, who had returned home. I was crying, telling her how much I missed Julie and how I wasn't sure I could live without her. I also shared what Catherine had told me and how I found it hard to believe some of the things she said. As I wiped the tears from my eyes, I suddenly saw a bright ball of light appear in front of me. It was so bright that I could barely look at it. Then, the ball of light disappeared, and in its place, imprinted on the side of my house, I saw angel wings and an apostle-looking man standing to the left of them.

I was describing all of this to my sister on the phone as it happened. She urged me to try and capture a picture of it with my cell phone, which I did. I was in shock, unable to believe what I was seeing. After about twenty seconds, the image of the angel wings faded away. I felt certain this was a clear sign from heaven that Julie was okay.

I had to let Catherine know what just happened. She said, "Well, that is a sign that is hard to miss." She told me to acknowledge that I had experienced it. She also said, "To me, it underscores your wife is a light being and very nearby. I noted it is outdoors and near flowers that Julie loved." Remember, Julie was always outside and did not like being inside the house. She was always planting something.

My interaction with Catherine did not stop there. I woke up at 8:17 a.m. on September 16 and was thinking in my head about what Catherine would want me to do to learn more about spirituality and mediumship. Next thing I know, Catherine, while I'm thinking about her, sends me a text with a link to a conference with the Institute of Noetic Sciences (IONS) on Facebook. I had never heard about this institute; I'll cover more about them in the next chapter.

Catherine lives in New Mexico, and I live in Virginia, so there's a two-hour time difference between us. Catherine isn't a morning person, so it was surprising when she texted me at 6:17 a.m. her time, which was 8:17 a.m. my time. What made it even more surprising was that I had just been thinking of her when she sent the message.

I responded, "Thank you so much. I was just thinking of you when you sent this to me. I know, when I say that's strange, you will say, no, it's not."

She replied, "That's because you are tuned in."

I'm receiving other signs from Julie as well. Sometimes, I can smell her perfume. One time, while my sister Linda was still visiting, I noticed a particularly strong scent of Julie's perfume. I asked Linda, who was sitting in the living room, to follow me into the hallway. As soon as she entered it, she said, "I can smell a strong scent of Julie's perfume." We assumed there must be a broken bottle of perfume somewhere, so we looked around but found nothing. After a few minutes, the smell faded away.

Since then, I've occasionally smelled her perfume in different areas of the house, along with the familiar scent of burnt toast. On the EVP, I've also been getting messages from her with words like "Love Alex."

One night, after my sister had gone back home, I was sitting in the living room with Beeps, the cat, praying and meditating. Suddenly, I felt a strange sensation come over my body, almost as if something was urging me to light one of Julie's candles. Julie loved all sorts of candles, though I myself had never been much of a candle person. I decided to grab one of her candles, place it on the coffee table in the living room, and light it. As I sat there, just watching the flame, I noticed that it seemed to dance around whenever I spoke.

At first, I thought it must be my breath causing the flame to flicker, so I walked away from the candle and started talking again. To my surprise, the flame continued to dance, even though I was far too distant for my breath to be affecting it. Determined to figure it out, I grabbed a towel and held it in front of my mouth as I spoke; once again, the flame danced around.

As I watched the candle's flame dance, I suddenly heard a voice in my mind telling me to take a picture of the flame with my cell phone. At first, I thought it was a strange idea—why would I want to do that? So I ignored it. But then I heard the voice again, urging me to take a picture of the flame. This time, I thought, *Okay, let me just do this so I can stop hearing it in my mind.*

I grabbed my cell phone and snapped a few pictures of the flame. When I looked at the images, I was struck by what I saw—Julie's face seemed to appear in the flame. It wasn't just my imagination; I was certain it was her face.

I decided to zoom in on the flame on the left to see the face more clearly. As I did, I could see it—it was my wife, Julie, with her blonde hair and beau-

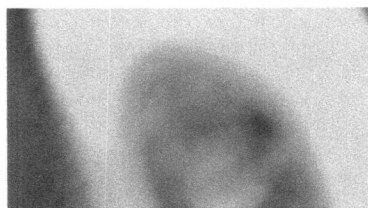

tiful face. I started crying in shock, unable to believe what I was seeing. I wondered if I was imagining it, especially given my grief and suicidal thoughts. I thought maybe I was seeing something that wasn't really there.

But to be sure, I sent the pictures to my sisters. When they looked at them, they also said it was Julie's face and hair. Their confirmation made it clear that I wasn't just imagining things—it really was Julie.

I'm struggling to understand what's happening—is it real or just my imagination? But there are too many things happening for it to be just a coincidence. Every day, I talk to Julie and spend time in the downstairs bedroom where she transitioned and went to heaven. I continue to pray and meditate, asking for signs from her.

One night, as I was sitting in that first-floor bedroom, talking to Julie, I suddenly saw a gold fairylike light flying around the room, right by the bed where she slept. It was an astonishing moment that left me even more uncertain about what was real and what was my imagination. But with everything that's been happening, I'm beginning to believe that these signs are real and that Julie is still with me in some way.

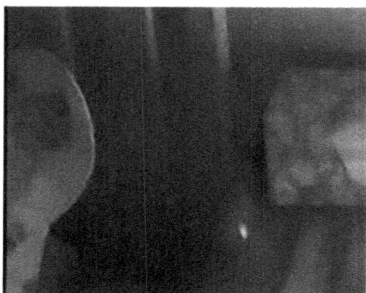

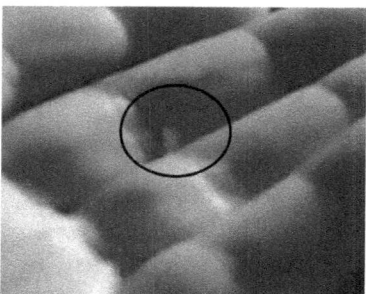

I began speaking to the little gold light as if it was Julie, telling her how much I love and miss her. I asked her to please stay with me and not leave me. Then, I said, "Julie, if that's you, please come to my hand, honey. I love you." To my surprise, the gold-light fairy moved toward my hand, and I felt a slight touch and warmth in my palm. It was an incredible, unexpected moment that filled me with a sense of connection and love.

I'm still in a lot of grief and struggling with thoughts of joining Julie on the other side, but my kids and Beeps are here for me. Beeps, the stray kitten who magically reappeared a week before we discovered Julie had stage 4 cancer, has been a constant companion. Julie knew how much I liked Beeps. While I loved all our animals, Beeps and I seemed to share a special connection.

After Julie passed, it struck me as strange how Beeps followed me everywhere I went in the house. If I went to the bathroom and closed the door, Beeps sat outside, waiting for me. When I fell asleep on the couch or bed, he was always right beside me. If I left the house, he sat by the door, waiting for me to come back home. It's as if he knew I needed him during this time, so he offered me comfort and companionship in a way that felt almost otherworldly.

One day, after getting out of the shower, I noticed that Beeps wasn't in his usual spot by the door. Instead, he was lying down in the upstairs hallway. I found it odd that he wasn't, as usual, in the bedroom with me while I was getting dressed. Then I noticed something on the hallway floor—a lighted image beside Beeps. It looked like Julie's face glowing softly in the light.

There was nothing in the hallway that could have cast a light like that. I was stunned and sent the image to my sisters. Both of them agreed—it was Beeps lying next to Julie. It felt as if it was yet another sign that Julie was still with us, watching over me and Beeps.

I was still smelling burnt toast in the mornings and catching the scent of Julie's perfume throughout the day. I missed her so much and wondered what else I could do to see her again. In my search for answers, I came across a wonderful lady named Sharon. I truly believe Sharon saved my life a couple of times when I was on the verge of joining Julie. I decided to visit Reverend Sharon, who is a certified master hypnotherapist, an advanced energy healer, an ordained minister, and an intuitive counselor. She offers a holistic approach to healing, focusing on the body, mind, and spirit. My goal was for her to hypnotize me so I could see Julie.

I know it sounds strange, and I even questioned how I would remember anything while under hypnosis. But I was desperate, so I told Sharon I wanted to be hypnotized to see Julie. Through tears, I also confessed that I had seriously considered joining Julie on the other side. Sharon suggested that before we try hypnosis, we should start with some energy healing. I had never heard of energy healing before and wondered what it was. According to Sharon, energetic healing touch is an ancient art involving the laying on of hands. It uses the energy field or aura that surrounds every living being. I was a little disappointed, but for some reason, I trusted her, so Sharon scheduled me for an energy-healing session.

While scientists have only recently verified this energy field, or aura, it has long been known to healers and mystics as the starting point of illness. Through this energy field, we have the power to heal ourselves and others. This therapy allows for healing on all levels—emotional, physical, and mental. It removes stagnant energy, recharges the chakras, and restores harmony and balance. I'll explain chakras a little later in this book.

I thought this all sounded pretty wacky and impossible, but Sharon seemed very intelligent, and as I mentioned before, I felt a strong sense of trust in her. I don't know why, but something inside me told me to trust her.

Plus, she had worked in the medical field for over twenty-four years, which gave her credibility in my eyes.

I went to see Sharon for the first time on September 26, 2023. I was a little nervous because, as a 100-percent disabled veteran, I constantly deal with hip and lower back pain. I was concerned that this could make things worse. Sharon had me lie on a very comfortable healing table in her office, and she began to work on me.

As she performed the energy healing, I started to feel an overwhelming sense of calm, and, remarkably, my pains seemed to fade away. The session lasted about an hour. When it was over, I got up from the table and noticed that my hip and lower back no longer hurt. In fact, I had no pain anywhere. I felt like a teenager again, free from the aches and pains that had plagued me for so long.

Equally amazing, during my session, Sharon was doing a mediumship reading while performing the energy healing. She said, "Julie says she loves you and is around you," and "Julie wants you to make her spaghetti sauce and spaghetti for the kids." Julie had learned how to make my mom's spaghetti sauce when we were stationed in Italy, and she had shown me how to make it many years before. I had made it a couple of times when she was busy.

Sharon also mentioned, "Julie wants you to do something with those two new bikes in the garage." Before Julie got sick, she had bought two new beach bikes for us to ride around the neighborhood. As Sharon relayed all this information, it felt as if Julie was right there in the room with us. I couldn't thank Sharon enough as I left her office—I was feeling so much better.

Naturally, I set up another appointment to see her. The second session was just as amazing as the first. But this time, something strange happened. As I was walking out of Sharon's office, I started seeing auras around everything—people, animals, plants, bushes, grass, and trees.

When I started driving home, I realized I couldn't figure out how to get there, despite being very familiar with the area. The drive to Sharon's office was about seventeen miles, and I had no trouble getting there, but on the way home, I was disoriented. I pulled into a gas station, called my sister Linda, and told her that while I could drive fine, I was seeing auras and wasn't sure where I was.

I punched my address into my cell phone's GPS, and it bizarrely showed I was 131 miles from home. I double-checked to make sure I had entered the address correctly, which I had. Ignoring the strange reading, I grabbed a Coke from the gas station and started driving again. I made it home, and it turned out to be the usual seventeen-mile drive, not 131 miles.

To this day, I still see Sharon and consider her a close friend. If she ever called me at 2:00 a.m. needing help, I wouldn't hesitate to jump out of bed to be there for her.

All of this still feels strange to me, especially given my upbringing in a conservative Catholic military family. None of these experiences were anything I had heard of growing up or during my adult life as a military officer. But I knew I had to find out more—to explore what else was out there that I hadn't been aware of and how it could help me stay connected with Julie on the other side.

Both Catherine and Sharon told me that Julie and I had been together in many past lives. This was a shocking idea for me, as I didn't believe in reincarnation—or at least, I thought I didn't. I even called my friend Todd to ask if he believed in reincarnation, and he said yes. All three of these people—Catherine, Sharon, and Todd—are very intelligent, kind, and loving. So I realized I needed to learn more before making up my mind about reincarnation.

CHAPTER 5

Seeking Answers: IONS, Reincarnation, LBL, and NDE

I'm still missing Julie and crying daily. I continue to pray, meditate a lot, and spend most of my days as I mentioned before—waking up, praying, and meditating until I fall asleep late at night. Due to a deep depression, I wasn't sleeping much during this time. It felt as if someone or something was guiding me through this period of exploration, almost as if I had a spiritual guide of some sort.

Julie began to come to me in dreams, but these were more than just dreams—they felt incredibly real. In the past, I have had vivid dreams and have awakened thinking, *Wow, that seemed pretty real*, but these dreams with Julie were on a whole new level of reality. One night, after she came to me in a dream, I began to question whether I had only dreamed she had passed. In another dream, the experience was so convincing that when I woke up, I knocked on my daughter's door upstairs and asked if she had seen her mom walking around.

According to Dr. Anne Reith, these types of dreams are often referred to as visitation dreams; we are visited by deceased loved ones who have moved "into the light." They can offer profound comfort. It's generally easier for spiritual entities—such as deceased loved ones, guides, or angels—to connect with us while we are asleep because that is when we are in a transitional state between our earthly existence and the spiritual realm. Our rational mind and ego are inactive, which allows us to experience things in our dreams that we might dismiss or overlook while awake.

This is where IONS (Institute of Noetic Sciences) comes in. IONS studies phenomena that are not yet fully understood by science. Before this journey, I had never heard of IONS, and when I started to investigate it more deeply, I was surprised by what the institute explores and researches. It opened up a whole new world of understanding for me.

A little bit about IONS, as I suspect many of you, like me, may not have heard of it before. The Institute of Noetic Sciences is a nonprofit scientific research center and direct-experience lab that specializes in the intersection of science and profound human experience. It was founded in 1973 by Apollo 14 astronaut Dr. Edgar Mitchell, inspired by a transformative personal experience during his space mission. IONS was created to explore the interplay between scientific knowledge and inner knowing.

The institute is driven by the belief in the power of science to explain phenomena that were previously not understood, harnessing the best of the rational mind to make advances that deepen our knowledge and enhance our human experience. A direct quote from their website states, "As scientists focused on what are common but not often understood phenomena, we are also aware of the vast historical records of wisdom practices that also speak to the mysteries and possibilities which allow us to access more of our human capacities."

When I first visited their website to learn more, I was still in a state of disbelief. I thought to myself, *Who are these scientists, and what are their credentials?* I clicked on the link to their staff page, expecting not to be impressed, but I was completely wrong. As I reviewed their qualifications, I found that many of the scientists held doctorates in fields like neurobiology, neurology, neuroscience, psychology, and physics. Their experiences before joining IONS were equally impressive.

IONS researches topics like psychic phenomena, intuition, channeling, energy healing, and much more—as an Army officer and a Catholic, areas I was neither familiar with nor believed were possible.

This exploration led me to start questioning the concept of reincarnation, something I had never believed in before. Why would we reincarnate? What is the purpose of reincarnation? Although I remained skeptical, I kept an open mind and began to investigate reincarnation more deeply.

I stumbled across, after some research, the University of Virginia (UVA) Division of Perceptual Studies founded by Dr. Ian Stevenson. Another thing I had never heard about, the Division of Perceptual Studies (DOPS) is a research unit within the Department of Psychiatry and Neurobehavioral Sciences at University of Virginia's School of Medicine. Dr Stevenson and DOPS have researched reincarnation cases for many years.

For the past forty-five years, researchers have explored young children's reports of past-life memories. These children often recount details of a recent ordinary life, and many have provided enough information to identify a specific deceased individual who matches their descriptions. These cases occur globally, though they are more commonly found in cultures that believe in reincarnation. The subjects are usually young children who begin describing a previous life around the age of two or three; this behavior typically stops by the time they reach six or seven years old.

Some children claim to have been deceased family members, while others describe being strangers from a different location. When they provide sufficient details, such as the name of the place, research scientists have often traveled there and identified deceased individuals whose lives seem to align with the children's statements.

Dr. Stevenson was particularly intrigued by the frequent occurrence of birthmarks and birth defects in children involved in reincarnation cases. Often, these physical manifestations corresponded to wounds—typically fatal—sustained by the deceased individuals whose lives the children claimed to remember.

In 1997, Ian Stevenson published *Reincarnation and Biology: A Contribution to the Etiology of Birthmarks and Birth Defects* (Stevenson, 1997a), an extensive two-volume work spanning 2,268 pages. This comprehensive study included reports and photographs of 225 cases involving birthmarks or birth defects. Many of these cases featured striking and unusual lesions, such as malformed digits, missing limbs, misshapen heads, and peculiar markings, rather than typical blemishes. In each case, the defects corresponded to wounds sustained by the deceased individuals.

Another aspect that intrigued Ian was the behavior of these children. He authored a paper examining the phobias exhibited by many of them. Their fears could often be linked to the manner of death from the life they claimed to remember (Stevenson, 1990a).

One reincarnation case that truly astonished me was the story of Sunny Ray. The couple in question had a son, whom I'll refer to as Michael. As a baby, Michael was obsessed with his father's Rolex watch, constantly reaching for it. When he could first speak, he pointed at the watch and declared, "Mine!" Eventually, he started calling himself Sunny instead of Michael. He insisted so firmly on being called Sunny that his parents eventually relented, and his mother affectionately started calling him "my little sunray."

Michael also made intriguing claims about his past life. He told his parents that he had a wife named Dawn and that they had lived in Texas. Although his current family primarily listened to classical music, Michael enthusiastically sang along to country-and-western songs, knowing the lyrics with surprising accuracy.

One day, while looking at a book about dogs, he pointed to a white spaniel and excitedly declared, "That's my dog, Willie!" Despite these peculiar details, his parents didn't seriously consider that Michael might be referring to a past life.

When Michael was seven, his parents attended a seminar in Texas; there, they met Dawn Ray. During a break, Michael's father chatted with Dawn and discovered she was a widow whose late husband was named Sunny. Shocked, Michael's parents invited Dawn to their hotel to discuss something important. They revealed that their son claimed to have been married in a previous life to someone named Dawn Ray from Texas. Dawn confirmed that she had indeed owned a white spaniel named Willie and that Sunny and Willie had been inseparable.

Determined to learn more, Mrs. Ray wanted to meet Michael. His parents arranged a flight for him, and, two days later, he traveled to Texas without knowing the details of the visit. Upon arriving, Michael was taken directly to Mrs. Ray's home. When Mrs. Ray opened the door, Michael immediately recognized her, calling out, "Dawn!" He ran into her arms, hugging and kissing her affectionately.

In the living room, Mrs. Ray, still skeptical, asked Michael if he recognized the house. He did not, prompting her to explain that she had moved in only two years after Sunny's death. Michael then inquired about his guitar. Mrs. Ray, astonished, retrieved the guitar from a cupboard. Michael played the instrument with surprising skill, despite it being slightly too large for him, and sang a familiar folk song. His parents were amazed, as they were unaware of his guitar-playing ability.

Michael also asked Mrs. Ray for his Rolex watch and camera. She produced the watch, which matched his father's exactly, and the camera, which perfectly fit his description.

I still had doubts, but I was slowly starting to believe in reincarnation. However, the question that now weighed on my mind was *why* we are reincarnated. I needed to understand the purpose behind it. Another concern was whether Julie would wait for me—would she refrain from reincarnating until I could join her? I had been told that Julie and I had always been husband and wife in many past lives, which brought some comfort, but it also raised more questions.

I also wondered why we don't remember these past lives if reincarnation is real. If we've lived multiple lives, why aren't those memories accessible to us? These were the questions that kept swirling in my mind as I continued my journey of exploration and discovery.

Next, I encountered the work of Dr. Michael Newton, who held a doctorate in counseling psychology and was a certified master hypnotherapist, as well as a member of the American Counseling Association. He was also a practicing psychologist with teaching positions at higher-education institutions in Los Angeles. Although he was initially skeptical about the metaphysical, Dr. Newton had repeatedly declined to conduct past-life regression sessions until he eventually decided to explore this area.

For those who might not be familiar with the term "metaphysical," it comes from the Greek phrase *meta ta physika*, meaning after the things of nature. According to the *Cambridge English Dictionary*, it pertains to the branch of philosophy concerned with understanding existence and knowledge. At some point in their lives, most people ask profound questions—for example, what is love, why am I here, and what is death?

Dr. Newton's journey into the metaphysical, particularly through his work in past-life regression, offered intriguing insights that challenged my own beliefs and opened up new possibilities for understanding the purpose of life and the nature of our existence.

Despite Dr. Newton's initial skepticism about past lives and his personal atheistic beliefs—views that later evolved—his extensive work with deep trance states in clients led to a groundbreaking discovery: life between lives (LBL).

"Life between lives" refers to the state between incarnations, where one exists as a spirit being. It also describes a process developed by Dr. Michael Newton. LBL is a profound hypnotic technique that allows individuals to recall their experiences in the afterlife, reconnecting them with their true selves and their guiding beings.

Based on consistent reports from thousands of clients across various backgrounds, Dr. Newton's research culminated in the development of a model of the spiritual realm. He documented the existence of and significant support provided by numerous higher beings in the "inter-life." These spiritual entities act as personal guides and teachers, assisting each individual through and between their lifetimes.

According to Dr. Newton, each of us has an immortal identity; we are far more than our physical form. We are a composite of experiences and lessons from countless past lives, each offering unique insights and growth opportunities for our eternal self's ongoing development.

In the late 1960s, Dr. Newton, using traditional hypnotherapy, treated a client suffering from psychosomatic shoulder pain. The man had sought hypnotherapy after medical investigations found no physical cause for his pain. Assuming that an unconscious trauma might be the root, Dr. Newton induced a deep trance and guided this man to the source of his discomfort.

The client relived a scene, from World War I, in which he was being bayoneted in a trench during the Battle of the Somme. Dr. Newton asked detailed questions about his military unit, commanding officer, and even the badges on his uniform, and then worked to desensitize the pain and resolve the issue. Although the client left feeling bewildered, he was healed.

Driven by curiosity, Dr. Newton later verified the client's story by contacting the War Records office in London, confirming the accuracy of his account. This pivotal moment had a profound impact on Dr. Newton and set him on a new path.

In 1968, Dr. Newton experienced the expanded life-between-lives (LBL) state for the first time while treating a woman with depression. By guiding her to the source of her pain, she naturally transitioned into the afterlife, where she encountered her soul group. This profound reunion addressed the deep sense of loneliness that had been at the root of her depression. During her LBL experience, she recalled having previously left her soul friends to learn independence. This experience resolved her feelings of isolation.

Dr. Newton began investigating the afterlife through careful research using his clients. It took him over twenty-five years to share his findings with the public, during which he developed a model of the spiritual realm based on insights from 7,000 clients over thirty-five years. His journey and discoveries are detailed in his best-selling books *Journey of Souls* and *Destiny of Souls*.

According to Dr. Newton, what is the purpose of our earthly incarnations? Each incarnation is designed to help us understand more about our true essence as a soul, our purpose for being here, and, sometimes, the relationships we have chosen for this life. For this reason, the planet Earth is often referred to as a school—the Earth school.

Some experiences on Earth are exhilarating, while others can be challenging; most of us encounter a mix of both throughout our lifetimes. Like those of any educational journey, all experiences in life serve a deeper purpose—facilitating profound personal and spiritual growth that we have chosen for ourselves. After our earthly life, the soul returns to the loving harmony of the afterlife.

Dr. Newton stated that souls appear to belong to a specific soul group from the very start of their creation. Members of this group often reincarnate together, sometimes at different times and in various places around the world. Eventually, these soulmates encounter each other at remarkable times and locations—a meeting meticulously planned by their soul group, but obscured by memory blocks once they begin their earthly journey. The mission for these souls is to fulfill their plans, face challenges, and experience these meaningful encounters.

Soulmates encountering each other at remarkable times and locations, as if planned, resonated with me. As you may recall from earlier, I met my wife while serving in the Army in Hawaii. It's incredible to think that a guy from Fayetteville, North Carolina, would cross paths with a girl from Paintsville, Kentucky, in such a distant place.

This perspective suggests that the complexity of life is less about random coincidences and more about a purposeful design orchestrated by a higher intelligence. A common theme in reports from individuals who have accessed the life-between-life state is the presence of a loving home awaiting us all. This is a realm characterized by pure, unconditional love, compassion, and harmony, where souls support and encourage one another in their growth and evolution toward higher consciousness.

We often reincarnate with certain members of our soul group, and there may be a central figure among them. We consistently seek out and reconnect with these individuals in each lifetime. Dr. Michael Newton does not use the term "twin flames"; instead, he refers to them as "primary soulmates." According to Newton, within our primary soul cluster, there are two types of soulmates:

> *Primary soulmates: These souls are someone with whom we have a profound connection, such as a spouse. It could also be a sibling, a close friend, or occasionally even a parent.*

> *Companion soulmates: These are the souls within our cluster group who form our spiritual family. Typically, they include parents, siblings, children, and close friends who play significant roles in our physical life.*

Is it possible that Julie and I have been together in many past lives and will continue to be together in future ones, as I've been told? This idea resonates with me because, the moment I met Julie, I felt as if she was the missing piece in my life. It felt as if we instantly loved and understood each other. If we had shared past lives and if our souls were aware of this connection, it could explain the deep familiarity and profound bond we felt when we first met.

While writing this book, I found myself briefly exploring my family history and discovered some intriguing parallels between my great-great-grandparents, Baxter Heaton and his wife, Susan, and my own life. Susan was a few years older than Baxter, just as Julie was older than I by the same number of years. Susan passed away before Baxter at roughly the same age that Julie did.

Baxter also had two older sisters named Caroline and Lydia—similar to my two older sisters, Carol and Linda. Whether this is merely a coincidence or something deeper remains a mystery.

Another question I have now is how religion intersects with the concepts of spirit guides and reincarnation. Reincarnation, which is central to many Eastern religions like Hinduism and Buddhism, suggests that after death, a person's soul is reborn into a new body to live another life. This notion of cyclical rebirth is not a part of biblical teachings. According to the Bible, the spiritual essence of a person goes to another realm immediately after death, as mentioned in Luke 23:43.

While I'm not a biblical scholar, a passage in which Christ discusses John the Baptist with his disciples might suggest that John the Baptist was considered by some to be a reincarnation of the prophet Elijah.

> *And his disciples asked him, saying, why then say the Scribes that Elijah indeed cometh, and shall restore all things; but I say unto you that Elijah is come already, and they knew him not, but did unto him whatsoever they listed. Even so shall the son of man also suffer of them. Then understood the disciples that he spoke unto them of John the Baptist. (Matthew 17:10-13)*

In other words, John the Baptist is viewed as the reincarnation of the prophet Elijah. Jesus Christ is said to have recognized the essence of Elijah in John the Baptist. It seems fitting that a powerful prophet would reincarnate to pave the way for the Divine Incarnation.

It was always part of Jewish belief that God would send his special messenger to men before the coming of the Day of the Lord.

> *And I will give power unto my two witnesses, and they shall prophesy a thousand two hundred and three score days, clothed in sackcloth. (Revelation 11.3)*

Scholars have varying interpretations of the two witnesses mentioned in the Scriptures. One perspective holds that they represent the witnesses of Christ's two comings. According to this view, Enoch and Elijah are identified as these witnesses. Traditional stories suggest that neither Enoch nor Elijah experienced death: Enoch "walked with God, and he was not, for God took him" (Genesis 5:24), and Elijah was "taken up to heaven in a whirlwind and chariot of fire" (2 Kings 2:11).

Proponents of this interpretation argue that Elijah is the witness of Christ's First Coming, having reincarnated as John the Baptist, while Enoch is believed to be the witness of the Second Coming, returning as a higher reincarnation before Christ's next return. It is worth noting that I had no knowledge of Enoch and had never heard of him before Julie's passing.

Another idea I've encountered is that heaven may have multiple levels. For instance, the Bible mentions a "third heaven" in 2 Corinthians 12. Additionally, many religious traditions describe various levels of heaven or the afterlife. For example, the Mormon Church (LDS) presents a view of the afterlife with multiple levels of heaven. The Book of Enoch depicts the patriarch Enoch's mystical journey through a hierarchy of ten Heavens, with Enoch traveling through the Garden of Eden in the third heaven before meeting the Lord in the tenth.

After learning about Dr. Ian Stevenson's and Dr. Michael Newton's extensive research into reincarnation and life between lives, my perspective on reincarnation, souls, and the levels of heaven began to shift. I started to consider the possibility that we are spiritual beings here on Earth, sent to learn and grow, with the ultimate goal of reaching a higher level of heaven or perhaps remaining in heaven permanently.

I often wondered if Julie, who was so extraordinary and loving, might be in a higher level of heaven, or perhaps doesn't need to reincarnate at all. Maybe her role in this and past lives as my wife was to help me improve and grow, which she certainly did in this lifetime.

I decided to research near-death experiences (NDE) as well. Unsurprisingly, many people have seized on NDEs as evidence of life after death, heaven, and the existence of God.

The descriptions of leaving the body and experiencing a blissful union with the universal often seem almost scripted from religious beliefs about souls leaving the body at death and ascending toward heavenly bliss.

I could rationalize in my mind that this common experience of leaving the body and ascending toward heaven might be due to the release of certain chemicals in the brain during death.

However, what truly intrigued me was the research of Dr. Bruce Greyson, a professor emeritus of psychiatry and neurobehavioral sciences at the University of Virginia. Dr. Greyson observed that some individuals who had near-death experiences were able to accurately describe events happening around them while they were clinically deceased. For instance, they could recount details about the actions of doctors and nurses or the conversations of family members and friends in the waiting room.

This led me to consider the possibility that during an NDE, a person's spirit might temporarily leave their body, allowing them to perceive and describe their surroundings from a different perspective. It challenged my previous assumptions and opened up new possibilities for understanding what happens at the threshold between life and death.

I also delved deeper into electronic-voice phenomena (EVP). While some might doubt that such programs and devices can capture messages from transitioned loved ones, I believe it's possible. Although EVPs aren't perfect, the appearance of specific words like "Alex Love," "Alex Forever," "Chip," "Avery," "Maria," "Axle," or "Alex Julie" at meaningful moments seems too significant to be purely coincidental, especially considering the timing. These occurrences have convinced me that there might be more to EVPs than mere chance, that they offer a way for those who have passed to communicate with us.

My research revealed that both Thomas Edison and Nikola Tesla were involved in attempts to create devices for communicating with "the dead"—Edison's term, not mine. I prefer "transitioned." By the 1920s, Thomas Edison had already cemented his legacy with ground-breaking inventions like the phonograph, motion picture camera, and incandescent light bulb. Despite his considerable achievements, Edison sought to develop one final ambitious invention: a "spirit phone" designed to communicate with the dead.

Edison's motivation for this new device was not only to advance science but also to outdo his rival, Nikola Tesla. Tesla, another remarkable genius and Edison's fierce competitor, in 1901, explored the possibility of contacting the dead while experimenting with a crystal radio powered by electromagnetic waves. Tesla's diary reveals his fear and fascination with unexplained signals he received, which he thought might be ghostly in nature. He later reported similar experiences with another radio, though he remained cautious, noting that the sounds resembled human voices speaking in an unknown language; he hesitated to conclude they were from beyond this world.

> *The day science begins to study non-physical phenomena, it will make more progress in one decade than in all the previous centuries of its existence.*
>
> *—Nikola Tesla*

CHAPTER 6

Reaching Out to Psychic Mediums and Discovering More

I'm still in a lot of pain, missing Julie more than I can put into words. In my grief, I started smoking cigarettes, and the thoughts of being with Julie continued to cross my mind every day. I can't stop thinking about doing something to join her. Despite this, she is still sending me signs and messages, and sometimes I think I can even hear her. The line between reality and the spiritual world feels blurred, and it's hard to make sense of everything that's happening.

It seems as if every time I get close to doing something to join Julie, either one of my sisters or a friend calls me, or my son stops by the house. And if that doesn't happen, I receive a message on the EVP device. Julie always tells me no and that she loves me. I know she wants me to stick around for our children and grandchildren.

At times, when I am in a really dark place, I can feel a warm chill come over me, and I know it is Julie reaching out to comfort me. I can sense her presence, but I miss so badly seeing her and holding her in my arms. The pain of her absence is overwhelming, even though I know she is still with me in some way.

I'm staying at our house, but I'm still not sleeping there most of the time. Most days, I'm either praying or meditating, and when I'm not doing that, I'm reading books on psychic mediumship. Sometimes, both day and night, I drive to parking lots just to sit and watch people. I get a little sad, but also happy for them, when I see couples walking together, holding hands.

When nighttime comes, I usually go over to my son's house and fall asleep on his couch. His better half, Summer, always puts pillows and blankets on the couch for me, and sometimes, if she thinks I look cold, she'll quietly throw a blanket over me while I'm sleeping.

I decided to call another psychic medium to see if they could also connect with Julie. I did a lot of research to find someone else I thought was credible. I'm still staying in contact with Catherine and Sharon, but I continue to have doubts about whether a psychic medium can truly get messages from your loved one. As I've mentioned before, I was the president of the Not Possible Club before Julie transitioned to heaven, so this is all still very new and challenging for me to fully accept.

I discovered a gentleman named Todd who is recognized as a psychic detective and medium. Todd began working at psychic fairs and providing personal readings in 2001. Todd has been involved in high-profile and serious-crime investigations, utilizing his psychic abilities to remotely perceive and interpret the energy of locations, even from hundreds of miles away. As a remote viewer, he can mentally visit locations as if he were physically present, gathering evidence that aids in solving cases.

I scheduled a mediumship reading with Todd toward the end of October. Todd seemed like a very easygoing person with a gentle tone of voice. He took a few seconds to connect with Julie and then told me she was at his house, looking around at pictures he had of horses and some older restored furniture—Julie loved horses and old furniture. He then told me that he had a strong connection with her.

Todd shared that Julie was worried about my back and the right-side leg pain I've been experiencing due to my back issues. He also mentioned that Julie still thinks I should get some chickens—a topic she had talked about for the last few years before she transitioned, as she wanted to put up a chicken coop on our property. He then told me that Julie was concerned about one of her cats named Kitty Girl. Right after Julie got sick, she asked me to take Kitty Girl to the veterinarian because she suspected Kitty Girl might be diabetic.

Todd then told me that a man was trying to communicate with me, and Julie had allowed him to come forward. He mentioned that this man had been in the Army, like me. I knew immediately that Todd was talking to my father. Todd then shared, in a joking way, that my father said, "Tell them not to water down my wine in the cellar."

Before my father passed, due to his heart condition, my mom and oldest sister, Carol—who was in Italy helping my mom—had been watering down his red wine before giving him a glass. After the reading, I called my sister, and both she and my mother were shocked because they had been doing that and hadn't told anyone.

I then asked Todd if I could communicate with Julie. He said, "Yes, you hear her, but she said you are focusing and trying too hard." Todd also said he could feel how much Julie and I loved each other, and it was very intense. I had heard the same thing from other mediums; some of them stated our love was so deep they would start to tear up.

Todd told me Julie said she was never going away and would always be with me until I joined her. He also told me Julie was very thankful to me for how I took care of her when she was sick. I always wondered what more I could have done to help Julie. Todd told me Julie does not want me to beat myself up on that; she said I had done a wonderful job taking care of her.

Todd, as well, then told me that I am a psychic medium. He said my ability is very strong, which he considered a good sign. Of course, I had heard this from Catherine, but I was still having a hard time believing it. I told Todd that I didn't think I was a psychic medium and asked why he was telling me this. He responded, "Because you are, and you just need to realize it." He added that my granddaughter Averie, Chip and Summer's daughter, was gifted as a psychic medium too.

I spoke to Todd a few more times over the next couple of weeks—sometimes to hear from Julie, other times to ask him questions about psychic mediumship. One conversation was particularly funny because I told him that sometimes I think I hear Julie replying to me, but other times I have a hard time connecting with her.

He explained that while grieving is natural after losing someone you love, it can sometimes make it harder to connect with them on the other side. Todd then suggested, "Just ask Julie about chickens and the different types of chickens, and she'll talk to you a lot." I found this suggestion amusing and very much in line with Julie's personality.

Todd told me, as other mediums had, that Julie and I had been together in many previous lives. He reiterated what Catherine had said—Julie and I are not truly apart; this is just a different and new phase of our relationship. "Love never dies," Todd said. "It continues on." He also mentioned that he had done a podcast after our reading, inspired by the love Julie and I share, titled "Love Never Dies."

Curious, I asked Todd how he connects with spirits. He told me that he had been able to do this most of his life, from the time he was born. He explained that he cleared his mind of all thoughts to make the connection. When I asked him how he does that, he admitted that he wasn't exactly sure—it was just something he had always been able to do.

At this point, I was becoming more curious about psychics, mediums, and remote viewing. I started doing more research and reading more books on the subject. It felt as if I was being guided by some unknown force throughout this process—an inner guide who seemed to understand what I thought and was leading me to explore these new realms.

As I continued my research, I came across the Central Intelligence Agency's (CIA) Gateway Process, which was entirely unfamiliar to me. Developed by the Monroe Institute in the 1970s, the Gateway Process is a training system designed to induce altered states of consciousness through meditation-like techniques combined with sound technology.

The scientific underpinnings of the Gateway Process are detailed in a twenty-nine-page report by US Army Lieutenant Colonel Wayne McDonnell, titled "Analysis and Assessment of the Gateway Process," which was written in 1983 and declassified in 2003. This report is believed to be part of the CIA's exploration into using the mind for Cold War espionage activities. Essentially, the Gateway Process aimed to alter states of consciousness in order to interact with nonphysical aspects of reality. According to the CIA report, its applications included converting energy to heal the body and traveling across space and time to access new information.

I was curious about the Monroe Institute and whether it still operates today, and it does. Founded by Robert A. Monroe in 1971, the Monroe Institute is a renowned center dedicated to exploring and experiencing expanded states of consciousness. For over fifty years, the institute has offered immersive programs that facilitate profound personal transformations, helping participants gain a new perspective on life and uncover a deeper sense of purpose.

The institute utilizes advanced Monroe Sound Science technology, guided imagery, and interactive group activities to support its programs. Individuals from around the globe and diverse backgrounds have attended, the only requirement being an open mind and a recognition that our existence transcends the physical realm.

In the wake of Julie's passing, I find myself grappling with questions I hadn't considered before. Is it truly possible for mediums to communicate with loved ones on the other side? I deeply desire to connect with Julie. Whenever I think about her with focus and relaxation, I experience sensations like chills and goose bumps, which feel reassuring and seem to indicate her presence. Occasionally, I feel as if I hear her voice in my mind, though I often question these experiences. Clearing my mind through meditation is still a challenge for me, as it's a relatively new practice, but I'm gradually improving.

The depth of my grief sometimes overwhelms me to the point that I contemplate joining Julie. These thoughts of suicide are becoming more concrete, and my military and supervisory training tells me that this is a serious sign that I need help.

I reached out to a local psychiatrist for help. He appeared compassionate during our first meeting and reassured me that grieving is a natural part of the process. He suggested practical strategies to help manage my grief, such as altering my routines—for example, changing grocery stores or shopping at different times. I explained that Julie and I used to do everything together, which makes these changes feel particularly challenging.

When I wasn't at work, I didn't want to play golf or hang out with the guys because I loved Julie so much, and she loved me just as deeply. We both wanted to spend our time together, doing things with each other. Julie often told me it was okay to go out and do those things, and I didn't see anything wrong with other men doing them, but for me, I just wanted to be with her whenever I had time off. Even at sixty years old, leaving work at five or six in the evening, I felt a rush of excitement and happiness as I walked across the parking lot, knowing I was getting into my car and heading home to her. As I drove closer to our house, that excitement only grew.

But without her, the grief and sadness felt as if they were getting worse with each passing day. The joy I used to feel coming home to her was replaced with an overwhelming sense of loss.

I started attending a grief-support group at a local church. According to grief-support literature, throughout this thirteen-week group, you'll discover what to expect in the days ahead and what's "normal" when grieving. Since there are no neat, orderly stages of grief, you learn helpful ways of coping with grief in all its unpredictability—and gain solid support each step of the way.

At my first grief-support group session, I found myself, besides the pastor, the only male among about seven women. Everyone was welcoming, so I decided to stay. Each week, we watched a thirty-minute video featuring experts discussing grief-related topics or sharing stories from those who had lost loved ones. After the video, the pastor led a group discussion. The sessions were grounded in Christian teachings, which was reassuring, though my perspective on certain aspects of passing had shifted since Julie's death.

I stopped attending after the sixth week of the thirteen-week program. Let me explain why—it was probably more about me than anything anyone did or didn't do. After one of the videos, a lady in the group asked the pastor, "What happens after our loved one dies? Are they in heaven or buried in the ground, waiting for the Second Coming of Christ?"

The pastor confidently answered that after death, everyone is waiting until the Final Judgment, after which they will be sent to either heaven or hell. He noticed me shaking my head no and asked, "Alex, what do you think happens after a loved one dies?"

I replied that as we begin to transition to the other side—to heaven—our loved ones who have already passed come to meet us. I then said that we are taken to heaven, where our spirits or souls live with other family and friends. I shared that before Julie passed, she was talking to her mother and father on the other side. I couldn't see them, but she could.

I could tell the pastor didn't necessarily agree with my answer. However, the ladies in the group started sharing their stories about how their loved ones had seen and spoken to family members who had passed before them, just as Julie did.

During the last session I attended, which was the sixth week of the grief-support group, another area of disagreement emerged. The topic was anger, and after the video, the pastor asked, "How many of you are angry at God?"

When it was my turn to speak, I stated that I wasn't angry at God. The pastor pressed further, asking if I was even slightly angry. I replied that I wasn't because I believed God would eventually reunite me with Julie, who had been a significant part of my life for thirty-nine years. To me, being angry at God didn't make sense. I also mentioned that after Julie transitioned, I had prayed for God to take care of her.

Somehow, the topic of reincarnation came up. One of the ladies in the group asked the pastor about it, and he stated that there is no reincarnation. The pastor then turned to me and asked, "Alex, what do you think about reincarnation?" I told him that I didn't believe in it for many years, but now I did. The pastor then asked me, "Will I, meaning me, the pastor, reincarnate as a frog?"

I replied, "No, not as a frog, but as a human."

With everyone in the group now focused on me, I shared information about Dr. Ian Stevenson and the Division of Perceptual Studies (DOPS) at the University of Virginia. I explained that DOPS has been researching reincarnation cases for decades, accumulating over 2,500 cases over the past fifty years. I suggested they visit UVA's website to explore the research for themselves and form their own opinions.

I returned to see the psychiatrist a few more times, but the conventional advice—everyone experiences grief at some point, focus on past hobbies, and grief will improve over time—wasn't helping me. While I now understand that grief does lessen with time, hearing that back then didn't provide the help I needed.

During one session, I finally blurted out to the psychiatrist, for reasons I still don't fully understand, "Doc, I know you understand grief after your mom passed from cancer when you were twenty-seven years old, and I appreciate you trying to help me, but I'm going to explore some other options." He looked at me in surprise and asked how I knew his mother had passed away from cancer when he was twenty-seven. I told him I didn't know—it just came to me.

I then told him, "I've been told, though I don't believe it, that I've been a psychic medium since birth." I also admitted that I was still thinking about suicide as a way to join Julie. He tried to explain why that was a bad idea and how it would impact my surviving family members.

I told him I understood all that, and that's why I was still here, but I needed something more. He then asked me if I had considered Ketamine treatment to help with the depression and suicidal thoughts. I hadn't considered it before, but I was familiar with Ketamine.

CHAPTER 7

Ketamine Treatment: Speaking to God

I'm considering doing Ketamine IV treatment. I was somewhat familiar with it because my son had undergone these treatments in his early twenties due to seizures related to epilepsy. The treatment had worked remarkably well for him, essentially eliminating his seizures. From his experience and what he told me, I knew that the treatment was somewhat akin to a near-death experience (NDE).

Knowing how it had helped my son, I began to seriously think about Ketamine IV treatment as a way to help with my depression and suicidal thoughts, hoping it might provide the relief and perspective I desperately needed.

I was still receiving signs and messages from the other side, especially from Julie. One day, while inside my house, I went to the bathroom and suddenly noticed green bars going down the wall. I stood there, staring at these green bars, wondering what on earth could be causing them. I had my phone with me, so I decided to take a picture. After a minute or two, the green bars disappeared.

Then I went downstairs to my living room, and to my surprise, the flat-screen, high-definition TV I had just bought—which had been working perfectly—had turned the same shade of green. I quickly took a picture of the TV, and just like on the bathroom wall, the green color disappeared after a minute. It was another puzzling sign, leaving me wondering what it all meant.

I was still seeing Sharon once a month for energy healing, and I showed her the pictures I took of the green bars and the TV. I always looked forward to my sessions with Sharon because, both physically and mentally, I felt much better after she completed the healing.

Sharon told me that the green color I saw was a message of love from Julie on the other side. She explained that green is the color of the heart chakra, and Julie was sending me love. I'll explain chakras in more detail later, but, basically, in our spirit self, we have these seven energy centers called chakras. At the time, this concept was bizarre to me.

Sharon also mentioned something that she felt might help me—the Harmonic Egg. She told me to contact a woman named Lynne if I was interested. Sharon recommended that I try the Harmonic Egg first, before considering Ketamine IV treatment. She believed that a session in the Harmonic Egg might help me and that I could possibly even see Julie while in it.

What is the Harmonic Egg? The Harmonic Egg/ Ellipse is a unique wooden, resonant chamber designed to deliver sound and light therapy to restore the body's balance and to enhance well-being. This egg-shaped chamber creates a tranquil and supportive environment that allows the mind, body, and spirit to deeply relax and release stress.

The inspiration for the Harmonic Egg/Ellipse came from Gail Lynn's personal journey with energy healing. After experiencing the benefits of a different resonant-energy technology, Gail, an engineer by background, envisioned a chamber with superior energy resonance. This drive to improve upon existing technologies led her to create a more effective healing tool. Her quest for healing knowledge led to the development of the Harmonic Egg, a groundbreaking chamber that merges advanced light and sound technologies with sacred geometry and Tesla mathematics.

I reached out to Lynne, the owner of the Harmonic Egg in our area, as recommended by Sharon. Lynne scheduled an appointment for me and asked what I hoped to achieve from the session. I shared with her the depth of grief and sadness I felt following the passing of my wife, Julie. When I arrived for my appointment, Lynne—a warm and caring woman, originally from the UK, who moved to the USA in 1984—spoke with me briefly.

I was unaware that Lynne possessed psychic and medium abilities, but she quickly sensed that I did as well. Despite my skepticism, Lynne confidently told me that I was a psychic medium.

I responded, "Oh no, I'm not." At that time, I was still struggling to accept, let alone believe, that I could be a psychic medium.

But Lynne just smiled and, in her British accent, assured me, "Oh, dear, yes, you are."

The session in the Harmonic Egg was wonderful. While inside, I decided to meditate and try to connect with Julie. A man appeared in my mind—I saw him as if I were dreaming, but I was fully awake. He told me that he was one of my guides. I acknowledged him but made it clear that I really wanted to speak to Julie. He laughed, understanding how insistent I was about connecting with her, and said we would speak later, as he had much to share with me.

I saw glimpses of Julie's face, heard her telling me she loved me, and felt her holding my hands. Of course, tears began flooding out of my eyes, and I didn't know why. I wondered if the flood of tears was part of the healing process.

After the session was over, I felt pretty good and positive. I scheduled my next session for the following week. At that time, I had already scheduled my first session for Ketamine IV treatment.

The next week, I saw Lynne again, and this time she had some things to give me. She began to mentor me without me really realizing it—and to this day, I will be forever thankful to Lynne. She handed me two sealed envelopes and asked me to tell her what pictures were inside.

I laughed and said, "How the heck would I know? The envelopes are sealed."

She laughed too and told me, "You can do this now—what are the pictures in the sealed envelopes?"

I hesitated and told her again I didn't know.

She encouraged me to take a breath, relax, and then tell her what I was getting.

I did as she asked and then told her that in the first envelope, there was a picture of a man and a little boy in a wheelchair, and in the next picture, there was a chair by the ocean.

Lynne smiled and told me I was very gifted, adding that I was also a healer.

I thought to myself, *Yeah, right—I can't even heal my finger that I jammed while working on my car.*

During my next session in the Harmonic Egg, I once again felt a profound connection with Julie and saw her in my mind. It was as if the reclining chair in the Harmonic Egg were detached from reality and floating freely. Though my eyes were closed, I opened them briefly and glimpsed Julie out of the corner of my eye to the left. Tears began streaming down my face unexpectedly, and

I couldn't understand why. It wasn't a conscious act; the tears seemed to flow as part of a healing process.

After the session, I mentioned to Lynne that I had a Ketamine IV appointment scheduled. Lynne, familiar with Ketamine, expressed concern that the session might profoundly affect me due to my alleged psychic and medium abilities. While I didn't fully believe in those abilities at the time, I couldn't help but wonder if there was some truth to her concern.

My oldest sister, Carol, who had just returned from Italy and hadn't seen me since Julie passed away, offered to accompany me to my first Ketamine IV session on December 7, 2023. Ketamine is primarily known as an FDA-approved anesthetic, but it has also been observed to have rapid antidepressant effects. While there is substantial evidence supporting Ketamine's effectiveness in treating depression, especially in cases resistant to other treatments, there is limited literature on its impact on grief-related disorders.

I was hopeful that Ketamine might alleviate my grief and suicidal thoughts; that expectation was inspired by an article on the National Institute of Health (NIH) website titled "Rapid Resolution of Grief with IV Infusion of Ketamine: A Unique Phenomenological Experience." This article described a case involving a twenty-eight-year-old graduate student who experienced complicated grief after the death of his wife due to obstetric complications. With the patient's and his family's consent for off-label use, he received a single IV infusion of Ketamine, which led to a unique experience that resolved his grief within minutes. In the NIH article, the individual describes his experience:

> *I was lifted by a chariot that flew at incredible speed and landed in what appeared to be a heavenly realm. The surroundings were filled with serene beauty and peace, and everyone was dressed in similar attire. I scanned the crowd, hoping to find my wife among those praying to the Lord. After a while, I spotted her at a distance, engaged in prayer. Overcome with emotion, I approached her and interrupted her prayers to speak with her.*

Ketamine IV infusion is often compared to a near-death experience (NDE) due to its similar effects. Accounts of NDEs are strikingly consistent, individuals describing intensely vivid sensations that feel more real than actual memories. Common elements include experiencing one's life flashing before their eyes, the sensation of separating from the body, observing one's own form from a distance, traveling through a tunnel toward a light, and feeling a profound sense of unity with a universal consciousness.

These descriptions align closely with religious concepts of the soul's journey after death and ascension to a state of heavenly bliss, leading many to interpret NDEs as evidence of life after death, the existence of heaven, and the presence of a divine being.

Since Julie passed, I'd stopped paying much attention to my diet. I used to try to eat healthily, mainly salads and fruits, but I had started just grabbing whatever was convenient, like cooked hot dogs from the local 7-Eleven, thinking that if I ate enough, something might change healthwise to bring me closer to Julie.

Carol drove down to my house the day before my Ketamine appointment, a two-hour journey from her place. While Carol was en route, we chatted on the phone. I asked what she'd like for dinner that night, and she replied, "Anything but hot dogs from 7-Eleven." I couldn't help but chuckle at her response.

One of my close Army friends, Tom, once told me, "Alex, you know they can sense on the other side what you're doing, whether it's smoking cigarettes or eating hot dogs." I responded with a bit of humor, saying I was just training to give Joey Chestnut, the Nathan's Hot Dog Eating Contest champion, a run for his money. Joey set the record by consuming seventy-six hot dogs in ten minutes during the contest on July 4, 2021.

My oldest sister, Carol, is an empath, deeply religious, and constantly immersed in the Bible. For those unfamiliar, an empath is someone who is highly sensitive to the emotions and feelings of others, experiencing them on a profound level. Carol avoids sad movies, songs, or even commercials, as they tend to affect her deeply. If someone starts crying, she's likely to follow suit, even if the tears are from a positive or happy moment.

Carol arrived at my house the day before my Ketamine treatment. We caught up on some things. I told Carol again about the strange signs I was getting in the house—most she was already aware of—just in case she saw or smelled something, so that she was not startled. I told her it was most likely Julie letting us know she was present.

I told Carol that I've been hearing church bells off and on and don't know why—there's no church or bells of any kind around where I live. I then told Carol random songs play in my head and was told by a medium to look up the lyrics of the song I was hearing because there was probably a message for me in them.

Oh, Carol met Beeps the cat also, and right away Beeps liked Carol. Kind of strange because other people had been by the house, and Beeps always sat next to me, but he went and sat next to my sister.

Carol asked me if I had been cooking at the house at all. I said no, just using the microwave. I'm a decent cook and used to cook when Julie was here. I told her I tried to use the dishwasher once and had to call Summer. When asked why, I told her I placed dishes in the dishwasher and then put regular dishwashing soap in the little container in the dishwasher until it was full. I started the dishwasher, and soap started coming out everywhere onto the kitchen floor. I grabbed towels and thought, *What the hell is going on?*

I called Summer and told her what was happening. She asked me if I used dishwashing soap for the dishwasher. I asked if there was a difference between the dishwashing soap you use in the sink and the one you place in the dishwasher. She said yes, laughed, and came by to help me clean up the mess. The good thing was the kitchen floor got cleaned.

So Carol and I talked that afternoon and evening. I think we got chicken salad sandwiches and potato salad from a local deli for dinner that evening. Beeps sat next to Carol on the couch as we talked. I told her how much I missed and loved Julie—which of course she already knew. I also told her what Lynne and Sharon had told me about being careful with Ketamine and what could happen because I was born with psychic-medium abilities. I told her I wasn't worried about that because I wasn't one.

While Carol was visiting me, I mentioned to her, after the lights in the room flickered, that Julie was with us. She asked me, "How do you know for sure?"

I told Carol, "I can feel Julie. She's touching my hand." I explained that I always feel a cold-breeze sensation above and on my hand when Julie is holding it. Sometimes, I just get goose bumps and a chill, like a fever in my body, when she's around me, but when she touches my hand, I specifically feel that cold breeze. Julie's hands were always cold for some reason, while I'm always warm, so that worked out well for both of us.

Carol seemed surprised when I told her this, so I asked, "Do you want to feel her touching my hand?" I then said, "Come over here, and place your hand right above mine."

Carol walked across the living room, placed her hand above mine, and said in amazement, "Wow, I can feel it."

Carol was staying in the bedroom upstairs that used to be Chip's, my son's. I asked her if she needed more pillows or blankets—something Julie would have done to make sure she was comfortable. I also told Carol that after Chip moved out and got his own place with Summer, Julie sometimes slept in his bedroom when I snored too loudly.

The next morning, as we were drinking coffee, Carol told me about something strange that had happened in the bedroom. She said she was watching TV before falling asleep and then turned it off with the remote. But a few minutes later, the TV turned back on. She said the remote wasn't even in her hands, and the TV had definitely been off before it turned back on.

I told her, "Julie always liked sleeping with the TV on and the volume low."

This wasn't the first time someone had an experience in that room after Julie went to heaven. Scott, who had been Chip's friend for many years and whom Julie and I considered our adopted son, had come by one night before Carol visited and offered to stay at the house with me. He slept in Chip's old bedroom. The next morning, Scott told me that during the night, he woke up freezing cold and felt as if someone was in the bedroom. After a few minutes, the freezing-cold sensation went away, and he went back to sleep.

I told Scott, "That was Julie visiting you in Chip's room."

Carol and I headed out for the forty-five-minute drive to the Ketamine treatment center. As I drove, a song kept playing in my head. The song was not one I'm familiar with. In my younger days, and even now, I listened to mostly rock music like the Eagles. I asked Carol to look this song up on her cell phone and read the lyrics to me. It was "Love Is the Answer," a song by Todd Rundgren. Carol of course started crying her eyes out while reading the lyrics, until she said she couldn't read any more. I asked her to save the lyrics on her phone so I could read them before walking in for my Ketamine treatment.

I went into the Ketamine facility, and they took me back to a room with a reclining chair-like bed. The nurse, a wonderful lady named Carolanne, knew me pretty well because she had given Chip his Ketamine IV treatments. They gave me headphones to listen to soft music with no words and a blindfold mask to cover my eyes.

As the Ketamine started entering my system, I began to feel as if I were sinking into the chair. Suddenly, I found myself in a dark tunnel with a white light at the end. Traveling through the tunnel made me feel a little nauseous. But as soon as I passed through the white light, I entered another world that looked like Earth but was cleaner and brighter. I saw people and angels; everyone seemed to know each other and to be incredibly friendly.

I called out for Julie and asked a few spiritual beings I encountered if they could help me find her. I thought I saw and heard her, but then some angels appeared and grabbed me; we flew upwards to what seemed like another planet or a different level of heaven.

This new place looked like a city made of gold, glowing with bright gold and white light. The angels took me to a structure that resembled a church or temple, unlike anything I had ever seen before. I had visited some magnificent churches in Italy and Germany while I was stationed there in the military, but this was on a whole new level.

I found myself standing in front of a gold altar with an extremely ornate gold decorative wall. Then, I heard a voice—calm and reassuring—and I instantly knew it was the voice of God, or at least what I believed to be God. The voice told me not to be afraid. When I asked God if I could please see Julie, He gently told me, "In time."

For some reason, I then asked God if we humans are the only ones He created or if there are others like us. He told me, "No, there are others I have created." He then showed me something like a pin-art image—the kind where you press your hand on an array of pins—and explained that each pin represented a planet He created for other forms of life or spirits.

When I asked if all these beings are like us, He said, "Some are like humans, some are a little different, and others are completely different." I then asked God if we were all created at the same time. God said, "No, some

I created well before Earth and humankind." He then told me something that struck me deeply. "Humankind, however, is the only one that has not learned their lesson after their First World War."

Desperate to see and speak to Julie, I told God how sad and in pain I was because of how much I missed her. He gently told me that He understood and that He feels everyone's sadness and pain. I admitted that I didn't fully understand. God then said, "Let me let you feel it for a little bit."

Suddenly, I was overwhelmed with the intense pain and suffering of the world. I saw and felt the anguish in places like Ukraine and Russia, Israel and Palestine, and in areas where people are starving and sick. The images were horrific, showing the suffering we, as humans, inflict on each other. It was a deeply intense, almost-unbearable experience.

Then, it stopped, and God asked, "Now do you understand?"

I was still in shock, feeling a profound sense of shame that we, as humans, cause God to feel all of that. He feels all of us, all the time—the good and the bad. I couldn't comprehend how, but I knew that He truly does feel all of us and what we do to one another.

God then said He needed my help—along with that of the others on Earth who were helping—to spread the message of love and peace.

I asked Him, "Why me, God? There are others, I'm sure, more worthy than me."

He kind of laughed and told me, "Why not you? You have been a good man."

God then took me to a bright-gold, very decorative wall and showed me a book embedded in it—the Book of Enoch. When He told me to read it, I asked how I would find this book. He said, "When you return, you will find it."

God, sensing that my mind was still focused on Julie, told me Julie was fine and in heaven with Him, and then He told me again to read the Book of Enoch. After I said that I would, angels came back and escorted me back to Earth and the Ketamine facility.

As I started to surface from the Ketamine treatment, I called out for Carol. She was already in my room and told me that she could hear me speaking to God. I told her that I needed to read the Book of Enoch. Carol's eyes widened, and she said, "Oh my God, I just ordered the Book of Enoch from Amazon yesterday."

I had no idea she had ordered the book because she hadn't mentioned it to me. I then asked Carol, "Who is Enoch?" She explained that Enoch is the great-grandfather of Noah.

Something strange happened to me after the Ketamine treatment. As I looked at Carol, I could see her aura. An aura is thought to be a luminous body that surrounds your physical one. To me, it looked like a cloud of different colors around her body—some colors were beautiful and vibrant, while others were darker and more greyish-black.

Carolanne, the nurse, overheard our conversation and asked if I could see her aura as well. I told her I could, and she asked me what I saw. I described her aura as having beautiful colors of pink, orange, and yellow, but also some light grey. She then asked me what I thought it meant. I told her she was worried about her father and his illness. Tears welled up in her eyes as she confided that her father had cancer and that she was indeed worried about him.

I hugged Carolanne, and then Carol and I left. On the way home, Carol asked me if I was still seeing auras around everyone. I said yes, but assured her it was okay. She asked if we needed to call Sharon or Lynne, and I told her no, but that we would if it didn't go away.

When we got back to my house, I was still a little dizzy from the Ketamine treatment. I told Carol that we had to find the Book of Enoch. She told me that we probably wouldn't find it locally and would need to order it from Amazon. But I insisted, saying, "God said I would find one today, and it has to have the same cover as the one He showed me."

Carol started searching all the bookstores within an hour's drive from where I live, and according to their websites, none of them had it in stock. I repeated that God said I would find one that day, so I started calling the bookstores myself. To my surprise, the Barnes & Noble thirty minutes away had just one in stock and said they would hold it for me.

As we were driving to Barnes & Noble, Carol asked if I could still see auras around people, and I said yes. When we arrived at the store, I tried not to stare at people's auras, but it was difficult. It wasn't what you would expect—in some cases, people who were well-dressed and looked friendly had darker auras, while people who looked a little rough had beautiful auras. I went to the counter, bought the book, and we left.

A little bit about who Enoch is for the folks who don't know—like me at that time. Enoch is a biblical figure who was a patriarch prior to Noah's flood, the son of Jared, and the father of Methuselah. The text of the Book of Genesis says Enoch lived 365 years before he was taken by God. The text reads that Enoch "walked with God: and he was no more; for God took him" (Gen 5:21–24). This has been interpreted by some scholars as meaning that Enoch entering heaven alive. He is a significant figure in various Jewish and Christian writings, traditionally regarded as the author of the Book of Enoch, and often referred to as the scribe of judgment. Additionally, Enoch is known as the great-grandfather of Noah.

Before Carol left to head back home, I asked her to take me to Chip's house. I wanted to talk to Chip about my Ketamine experience. I was a little upset that he had not explained or told me about it in enough detail beforehand. When we got there, Carol started chatting with Summer and playing with Avery and Avery's half-sister, Parker, whom she brought Barbie dolls.

I approached Chip and suggested we step outside and talk. Once alone, I said to him, "Man, you didn't prepare me for the Ketamine experience."

Chip, who had undergone about six Ketamine treatments to manage his epilepsy, responded, "Dad, how can you explain something like that to someone who hasn't experienced it?" He made a valid point; it is challenging to convey the experience in detail.

I then asked Chip, "Did it feel more real on the other side or more real here?"

He replied, "Definitely more real on the other side while under Ketamine."

I nodded in agreement.

After Carol left later that evening, I started reading the Book of Enoch. I initially thought it would be a difficult read, but as I continued, it seemed as if I had read this book in the past; I understood what I was reading. The words in the book just flowed to me.

In the Book of Enoch, God is called the Lord of Spirits. This makes sense to me since I believe we are all spirits. It also speaks about the ten levels of heaven associated with the celestial realms and the hierarchy of angels. Could reincarnation be associated with the ten levels of heaven and our spirits/souls coming back to learn and grow on Earth to achieve a higher level of heaven, the ultimate goal being level ten where God resides, the place of ultimate divine glory and majesty?

CHAPTER 8

Hearing Church Bells:
Seeing an Angel and a Shaman

The Ketamine seems to be helping with my thoughts of joining Julie, but I still miss her terribly and cry multiple times throughout the day. It's the middle of December 2023, and I don't feel much like celebrating Christmas without Julie. To say that Julie went overboard on Christmas with both the decorations and gifts would be an understatement.

I used to tease Julie as she put up Christmas lights around our house, joking that they could probably see our house from space. My December electric bill certainly backed that up. Julie just loved Christmas. I think part of the reason was that, as a child growing up in the Appalachian Mountains, her family didn't have a lot of money, so Christmas gifts were very few and mostly practical, such as clothes that were needed.

I loved Julie, so what made her happy made me happy. If she wanted to go all out during Christmas, so be it. And it wasn't just us—our dogs, cats, squirrels, rabbits, birds, and even some of the neighborhood pets and children got Christmas gifts from Julie as well. She had such a big heart and wanted everyone, human or animal, to feel the joy of the season.

I'm still receiving signs from Julie and the other side. One day, I was outside, and it was an unusually comfortable day for winter. I was standing in the front yard, where Julie loved to plant flowers, when I saw what looked like the image of a shaman. I quickly took a picture, and the image disappeared twenty to thirty seconds later.

I couldn't help but wonder if I was seeing something that wasn't really there. But, to me, it truly looked like a shaman. I sent the picture to my sisters, and both of them agreed—it looked like a shaman to them as well. This experience made me recall that both our parents told us that Julie and I had Native American blood. It was as if this connection was manifesting in ways I hadn't expected, adding another layer to the signs I'd been receiving.

A little bit about shamans and shamanism. Both were explored by Stanley Krippner, a renowned American psychologist and pioneer in consciousness studies. According to Krippner, shamans are "community-designated spiritual practitioners who intentionally alter their consciousness to access information from the spirit world. They use this acquired wisdom and power to aid and heal both individuals and their entire community." Krippner further described shamans as the original physicians, diagnosticians, psychotherapists, and religious leaders.

I'm still not sleeping in the master bedroom upstairs where Julie and I used to sleep because it's too hard for me without her physically there. Most days, I spend my time praying and meditating, then head over to Chip and Summer's house. Late in the evening, I drive back home to sleep on the couch with Beeps.

One night, I left their house around 10:30 p.m. Though they both offered me a place to stay, I declined, feeling a strong urge to return home, where I believed Julie's presence was with me. As I drove down a dark, tree-lined road near my house, a large owl suddenly landed in front of my car. I slammed on the brakes, skidding to a stop.

The owl remained on the road, unmoving. Assuming it must be feeding on something, I got out of the car to investigate but found nothing. Standing there, the owl and I locked eyes for a few moments before it eventually flew away. I returned home, pondering the encounter with a sense of wonder, as I had never seen an owl around my area before.

I then remembered that one of the spiritual people I had been talking to mentioned something about the spiritual meaning of seeing an owl. I decided to look it up on the internet and found that an owl crossing your path often signifies a big change is coming. The owl is considered very spiritual and is often seen as a sign from angels or spirits. It seemed strange, but a big owl had just caused me to lock up the brakes on my car and had stared me in the eyes for about five minutes.

For some reason, that night, I decided to sleep upstairs in the master bedroom for the first time since Julie transitioned and went to heaven. I went upstairs to the bedroom and lay down in bed, leaving a small light on, as we used to do in case one of us needed to get up and go to the bathroom.

As I lay there, still wide-awake, I suddenly saw the shaman figure in the bedroom—the same one I had seen outside. At first, it freaked me out a little and startled me, but as I watched, the shaman appeared to be performing some sort of ceremonial dance, gently bobbing his head up and down.

I no longer felt nervous or scared and just watched him. It was surprisingly relaxing and calming to watch the ceremonial dance, and I eventually fell asleep. The next morning, I woke up feeling different—there was a strange but wonderful sense of love and peace within me. I wasn't sure what was going on, but I had this overwhelming feeling of loving everyone.

As Christmas Day approached, I still wasn't in the mood to celebrate, but I knew Julie would want me to, especially for the children and grandchildren. So I decided to head out and buy some gifts. It wasn't easy walking around the stores without Julie by my side.

A few days before Christmas, I started hearing Julie's voice in my mind, off and on, asking me to please make

Christmas dinner for everyone. I told her, in my mind, that I couldn't do it, that I wasn't up to it. But she kept gently insisting, knowing that eventually, as always, I would do what made her happy. She did say it would be okay to cheat a little and get some of the food from the Honey Baked Ham store. So I called Chip and asked him to ride out to the store with me, and he agreed.

When Chip arrived at my house and got into the car with me, I asked him, "Do you hear those church bells?"

He looked at me and said, "I don't hear any church bells, Dad."

But I kept hearing them, clear as day. We drove to the Honey Baked Ham store and picked up a bunch of food. Yes, I still made some food from scratch—and, no, this time I didn't use the wrong dishwashing detergent afterward.

As we were leaving the Honey Baked Ham store in a crowded part of town, I spotted a man begging for money at the intersection. I decided to stop and give him a twenty-dollar bill to help out. As we pulled up, I rolled down my window and handed him the money. Immediately, I noticed he was wearing a large, beautifully adorned cross with vibrant gemstones. The man looked as if he could have stepped out of a daytime soap opera—tall, around six two, with blond hair and impeccably straight white teeth. He accepted the twenty dollars, blessed Chip and me, and began speaking about how God loves everyone and desires us to love one another.

When the light turned green, he returned the twenty dollars, blessed us again, and reiterated that God loved us. As we drove away, Chip remarked that the man's voice had sounded as if we were in an auditorium. I agreed, feeling certain that he was no ordinary person but an angel. We both glanced back, but the man had vanished.

Before Christmas, I had another session at the Harmonic Egg. I was excited to go and couldn't wait to see Lynne, who was very spiritual. As I removed my belt and shoes before getting into the egg, I sat down with Lynne and told her about the owl. She said that it's normally a sign of a spiritual awakening. I then told her about the shaman. She said she felt he was there to help heal me and that he was one of my spiritual guides on the other side.

I then told Lynne about the homeless man. Lynne, when she's not working at her Harmonic Egg business, also works at a shelter for the homeless. After I explained everything to her, she smiled and said that he was an angel. She laughed and added, "I've never known a homeless person who gives you your money back." Then she told me something that took me by surprise. "Besides being a psychic medium, Alex, you are also a healer."

I asked Lynne, "Who can teach me how to heal?"

She told me about a wonderful lady named Denise, a Reiki master and shaman, who also teaches healing. Lynne said Denise could help me explore and develop my healing abilities.

CHAPTER 9

What the Heck is Going On?

As the new year begins, I'm still hearing church bells, but some other things are happening as well. I'm still in a lot of pain and grief over Julie. I miss her so much. I start to wonder if I may be a psychic medium and healer. I decide to practice clearing my mind of all thoughts, just as Todd had mentioned. I also decide to start attending a Metaphysical Church in the local area—something I had never heard of before.

A Metaphysical Church is essentially an interfaith organization. They welcome people of all faiths and invite everyone to join them on their spiritual journeys. They believe in God, the divinity of each person, and the sacredness of nature. They also believe in the power of prayer and that spirit is active in our lives, offering wisdom and guidance directly from angels and spirit guides.

It sounded kind of strange to me, but I thought I would give it a try. I felt comfortable right away at the Metaphysical Church I attended, especially after hearing the Our Father prayer, and everyone was so kind and welcoming.

I decided that I needed to get a crystal, thinking it might aid in my spiritual journey. Julie had a collection of crystals, but I couldn't find where she had hidden them. She was deeply spiritual, and I had always thought that crystals, tarot cards, psychics, and natural healing were rather farfetched.

In fact, when I first spoke to Catherine, the medium who was also a math teacher, she asked me, "Alex, you think all this is wacky, don't you?" I admitted that, yes, I did think so at the time, though I was beginning to open my mind to these ideas due to the signs I had been receiving and the research I had done.

I drove to a local store that sells raw crystals. I had read online that you should see which crystal you feel drawn to, so I asked the young man behind the counter if I could move my hand over the crystals to see which one I felt connected to. He said yes. As I ran my hand over the many crystals in the store, I felt a subtle pull toward one of them, so I bought it and took it home.

When I got home, it was sunny outside, so for some reason, I decided to look at the crystal against the light. To my surprise, I saw what appeared to be the image of a lady inside the crystal. Startled, I called the crystal store and asked if they etched images into the crystals. They, of course, said no and asked me why. I told them that there was an image of a lady etched into the crystal I bought. They asked if I wanted to bring it back, and I said, "Heck no."

I'm still receiving signs from Julie. I can smell her toast and coffee in the morning and her perfume through-out the day. When I'm really sad and crying, she seems to send me mes-sages through the EVP device. It's always "Love Alex" that magically appears when I'm especially down.

One day, however, something par-ticularly surprising happened. I was over at Chip's house. He was at work, and Summer was home with Avery, my granddaughter, who was about a year and a few months old at the time. I was on the floor, playing with Avery, and I had the EVP device right next to us. No one was talking. Suddenly, the word "Av-ery" popped up on the screen as I sat there playing with her. I showed Summer, and we were both amazed. What are the odds of that word randomly showing up at that exact moment?

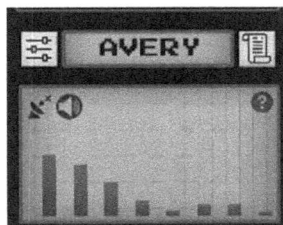

Strange things have also been happening during my meditations. I've started seeing vivid images of Julie and other scenes that feel incredibly real. Sometimes, it feels as if I'm traveling to different places—one moment, I'm walking through a forest; the next, I'm in a shopping-center parking lot. What's odd is that when I'm in these places, I can see other people and move around, but they don't seem to notice me.

Curious and a bit unsettled, I called Lynne to ask what might be going on. She calmly explained, "Your third eye is opening."

The third eye, located in the center of the forehead, between the eyebrows, is associated with intuition, insight, and spiritual awareness. As the sixth chakra in the body's energy system, it plays a key role in balancing the body, mind, and spirit. When the third eye is open, it can lead to heightened states of consciousness and even out-of-body experiences, offering deeper insights and self-awareness.

I'm not sure what is going on and what I need to do to figure all of this out. I started to go back to my job on the military base part-time. One day, while sitting in my office and talking to Pat, one of my division chiefs, I heard Julie tell me to call Chip. He works as a land surveyor and was surveying. I told Pat to hold on for a minute, and I called Chip. I asked, "Chip, are you surveying near water today?"

He responded, "Yes, Dad. How did you know?"

I replied, "Mom told me, and she wants you to be careful since you don't usually survey around water when it's this cold." Pat looked at me in surprise, and I apologized, saying, "Sometimes Julie communicates with me like this."

Another strange thing that has been happening is a portal occasionally opens up in my house by the living room wall, right behind a lamp. The portal stays open for just a minute and then disappears. The face I see in the portal looks like my grand-father on my father's side. When the portal isn't there, it's just a blank wall behind the lamp with its three bulbs, as you see in the picture. The first time this happened, my instinct was to run out of the house. But I didn't feel threatened, so I just sat there until it went away.

A few days later, something else strange happened. I was in the local grocery store when I thought I heard a lady's voice, in my mind, urging me to go up to her son. Her son looked to be around thirty-five years old and was wearing a hospital medical-staff uniform. I tried to ignore the voice, but she was persistent, so I finally approached him. I said, "Excuse me. I'm sorry to bother you, but I'm getting some messages from your mother. Would you like me to share them with you?"

After he said yes, I told him that his mother was a schoolteacher who had passed from breast cancer, that she loved to hug people, was very active in the church, and sang in the choir. I also told him that she was with her mother, who had passed about a year before she did. Lastly, I conveyed her message that she loved him very much and still visits him. He thanked me, shook my hand, and we parted ways.

Right after that, I left the store without finishing my shopping. As I sat in the car, I asked myself, "What the heck is going on with me?"

Feeling the need to understand more, I did some research and came across a contest, sponsored by Robert Bigelow, on evidence of life after death. Mr. Bigelow, a billionaire who owns Budget Suites of America and is the founder of Bigelow Aerospace, has provided financial support for investigations into UFOs and parapsychological topics, including the continuation of consciousness after death.

The 2021 essay contest was a significant global initiative aimed at exploring the evidence for life after death. Winners were selected based on the strength and persuasiveness of their arguments, focusing on whether they could convincingly demonstrate, beyond a reasonable doubt, the survival of human consciousness. The judging panel consisted of seven independent experts, ensuring that neither Robert Bigelow nor the staff of the Bigelow Institute for Consciousness Studies (BICS) influenced the outcome.

The contest attracted global interest, garnering 1,300 submissions from all over the world. Ultimately, 204 essays, each up to 25,000 words long and representing thirty-eight countries, were submitted. Seven distinguished experts reviewed these essays and selected twenty-nine winners who were awarded a total of $1,800,000 at a gala event in Las Vegas in December 2021. This contest was a pivotal moment in the field; it established robust evidence for the survival of human consciousness beyond physical death.

Dr. Jeffrey Mishlove emerged as the winner; he is the holder of an interdisciplinary doctoral degree from the

University of California, Berkeley, earned in 1980. As a licensed psychologist in California, Dr. Mishlove's essay presented compelling evidence for the survival of human consciousness after death.

One issue that troubles me now, especially after exploring reincarnation and life between lives through Dr. Newton's work, is the possibility that if I ended my life before my time, I might not have learned the lessons I was meant to learn. This could potentially mean I'd have to return and relive Julie's transition to the afterlife all over again. I certainly don't want to find myself stuck in a Groundhog Day scenario like the one in the movie with Bill Murray.

I'm still praying and meditating every day, and now the sounds of church bells are pretty constant in my ears. I decided to schedule an appointment with my primary medical doctor on the Army base. I got an appointment and went in to see him.

I told him that I have a constant ringing in my ears. He did an examination and asked me when it started. I told him it began a few months after my wife went to heaven. He asked if I had been to any loud concerts, been around any heavy machinery, or done any shooting of guns since Julie passed. I told him no.

After examining me, he said he didn't see anything wrong but suggested we do some lab work to make sure everything was okay. He assured me that he would call if anything came up.

I decided to be open with the doctor and asked if our conversation would remain confidential, as per doctor-patient confidentiality rules. He assured me it would. So I shared that I had been hearing church bells and that I had been told I was a psychic medium. Not surprisingly, he laughed and said he didn't believe in such things. I admitted that I hadn't believed in them either for most of my life.

He then asked me what I was sensing from him. I explained that it wasn't something that could be rushed and that I needed time to pray and clear my mind. Despite my response, he insisted, with a smile, that I share what I was picking up. Although I felt his reaction was somewhat dismissive, I tried to understand his perspective.

I then told him I was sensing his father, who was nearing the end of his life. I mentioned that his father had stage 4 cancer and was in hospice, his mother there caring for him. I also shared that his father would help many people after he passed because he was a minister. The doctor was astonished and repeatedly asked how I knew this. I explained that this was part of my psychic-medium abilities.

A few days later, I received a call from the Army hospital. Expecting bad news that might mean I could soon be with Julie, I answered with joyfulness. However, the doctor informed me that he had not found anything significant, but he was still surprised by the accuracy of what I had sensed. He mentioned that he had shared my insights with his wife and asked if I would help him connect with his father after he passed. I agreed to do so.

Carol had gone back to Italy at the end of December and wasn't planning to return until the middle of February. While she was in Italy, I did some readings for my mom to deliver messages from my father. On December 30, 2023, while Carol was in Italy with our mother, I called them on the phone. My mom asked Carol to ask me if my father was in the house with them.

I said, "Let me check." I couldn't feel his presence there and then realized he was with his sister in North Carolina because she was ill and nearing her transition. My father had always been very close to his sister Elise, so that didn't surprise me.

When I told Carol, she responded, "Oh no, no one has contacted me about Elise." I had lost touch with my aunts, uncles, and cousins in North Carolina when I joined the Army, but my two sisters had stayed in contact with them over the years.

A few days later, Carol received a message from our cousin, after reaching out to ask about Aunt Elise, who said, "I haven't had an update since the weekend, but she's at Amy's"—her daughter's—"on hospice. The doctors said there's nothing more they can do for her. When they tried to treat her heart, it affected her kidneys."

After sending me that message, my sister Carol then asked me, "Dad was with her the other night?"

I said, "Yes, she can see Dad, and it's comforting to her."

On January 16, 2024, my father helped Aunt Elise transition to heaven.

Carol returned from Italy in February and took me to another Ketamine IV infusion because I was still having periods in which I missed Julie so much that I wanted to be on the other side with her. When we got to the Ketamine IV place, the process was pretty much the same as the last time: headphones to listen to soft music, eye covers, and lying back in the reclining chair until the Ketamine kicked in, which didn't take long at all.

As before, I traveled through a tunnel, saw a bright light, and came out on the other side. Once again, I was frantically looking for Julie. I saw her and started running towards her, and she smiled at me just before the angels grabbed me.

The angels took me inside what looked like an Egyptian pyramid, but it appeared newly built. Inside a chamber-like setting within the pyramid, I looked up at hieroglyphics. The angels then, telepathically, told me, "Now, you understand."

I replied, "No, I don't understand."

The angels said, "Yes, you do. Remember."

I looked at the hieroglyphics again and told them I didn't understand. I then asked the angels to take me to Julie.

They responded, "You are Julie, and Julie is you, and you will always be together."

This didn't make sense to me.

They then showed me a beautiful, extremely large tapestry decorated in red and gold colors. They told me that each of us is a small thread in the tapestry and that we are all connected. That actually kind of made sense to me, though I wasn't entirely sure why.

The angels then took me to a very ornate auditorium. As I sat there looking around, I was suddenly showered with an incredibly bright gold-and-white light. It felt amazing—soothing and healing. I could feel an intense, overwhelming love emanating from the light, enveloping me in a sense of pure, unconditional love and healing energy.

I called out for my sister Carol. Carolanne, the nurse, came into the room, and I asked her to please get my sister Carol. I felt an urgent need to share this experience with her.

Carol came into the room, and I asked her to hold my hand. As she did, I saw the gold-and-white light travel down my arm, into my hand, and flow into her body. In my mind, I saw my sister glowing as she received this light from me. I asked her if she could feel it, and she said yes.

Hearing what was happening, Carolanne asked if she could feel it too. I agreed and asked her to hold my hand as well. Carolanne had been worried about her father's illness, and as she held my hand, the same thing happened. The gold-and-white light flowed from my body into hers.

After this, I found myself fully back in the auditorium on the other side, being showered with the light. The light began to fade after some time, and I eventually returned to the Ketamine facility.

As I came around from the Ketamine session and started to regain my bearings, I told Carol about being taken to the pyramid and the angels asking me if I understood the hieroglyphics. I admitted that I told the angels I didn't understand. Carol then shared that some believe Enoch built the pyramids with the help of angels. I was stunned.

Eric von Däniken explored the writings of an ancient Arabian historian named Al-Maqrizi, who claimed that the Great Pyramid was built by a pre-Flood king named Saurid. This king—also known as Enoch in Hebrew tradition—was thought to have constructed the pyramids as a safeguard for biblical texts intended for future generations. According to von Däniken, the technology used to build the pyramids was provided by advanced beings with whom Enoch was in contact.

I then asked Carol and Carolanne if they had felt the healing gold-and-white light when they held my hand. They both said they did, and I could see a look of surprise and happiness on their faces. Carol said it felt as if a comforting, cool energy were flowing through her chest, calming her down.

At a later Ketamine session, to which my son, Chip, drove me, the same thing happened with the shower of gold-and-white light. I called Chip into the room and asked him to hold my hand. Later, I asked if he had felt anything, and he said yes—a calm burst of energy was flowing through his body as I held his hand.

I started offering what I call angelic healing to family and friends. The process is still a bit unclear to me—essentially, I meditate and pray to God and the angels, visualize gold-and-white light, and then focus on sending healing energy to the person who requested it. The next day, people often tell me that their pain—whether it's from their back, joints, knees, shoulders, or even illnesses like a cough or flu—has disappeared. I'm astonished by these results and always remind them that it's not me but the angels who are working on their behalf.

Despite these experiences, I struggle to ask for healing for myself, believing that my role is to help others, not myself. Even though I realize this doesn't make much sense, I can't seem to shake the feeling. I keep asking myself, "What the heck is going on?"

At this point, after all that I've seen, nothing really freaks or weirds me out—or so I thought. One day, the mirrors in my house start fogging up, and I can see what appears to be Sanskrit words forming in the mist. At first, I thought it was just my imagination, but the fog and words disappeared from the mirrors after a few seconds. Curious, I decided to take a picture of one of the Sanskrit words the next time it happened, just to see if that was indeed what I was seeing.

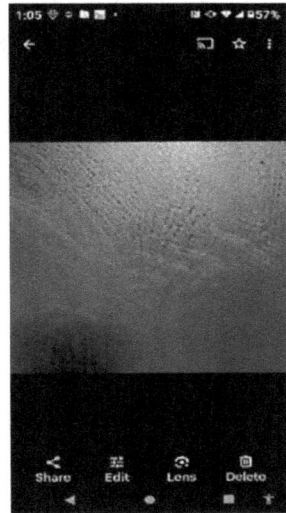

I sent the picture to my sisters and asked them what they thought. Both of them confirmed that it looked like a Sanskrit word to them. I showed it to my son as well, and he saw the Sanskrit word too. Unsure of what all this meant, I decided to look up Sanskrit and its significance.

Sanskrit developed out of earlier Prakrit languages between the 100 BC and 200 AD, with the earliest Sanskrit inscription dating to around 150 AD. Christianity was first brought to India during the first century AD by the Apostle Thomas. To this day, I don't know why Sanskrit words randomly appear on the mirrors in my house. Given the strangeness of it all, I decided that I need to seek help from trained professionals who might be able to provide some insight.

CHAPTER 10

Wait, What? I'm a Psychic Medium? You're Crazy.

A t this point, I'm starting to think, *What if I really am a psychic medium with the ability to heal?* I realize I need someone to help train me in both. By now, I've read quite a few books on psychic mediumship and believe it's possible to communicate with our loved ones on the other side. I think we are spirits in human bodies, and those who have transitioned are spirits too, so perhaps it's possible to have spirit-to-spirit communication.

I'm not entirely sure how I'm receiving messages from my father and Julie, but I am. However, connecting with Julie is still very difficult for me because of the intense grief and sadness I feel over her transition. You'd think she would be the easiest one for me to connect with, but I believe the grief and crying make it harder.

I need to clarify something that I didn't know early on: all mediums are psychics, but not all psychics are mediums. This can be confusing because many people offer both psychic and mediumship readings, sometimes in the same session.

A psychic uses their intuition to receive information about someone's past, present, future, or all three. A psychic reading may offer guidance, inspiration, fresh perspectives, or strategies for dealing with challenges. These readings might involve predictions, insights into what's happening in your life, or analyses of your career, finances, or love life.

A medium, on the other hand, connects with someone's recognizable loved ones in spirit and provides enough detailed evidence to show they're truly linking with a specific individual. It's all about communicating with those who have transitioned. In other words, a medium is someone who can communicate with souls/spirits on the other side.

At this point, I'm searching for a certified medium who can bring messages from Julie and can help train me. I reach out to a wonderful and beautiful lady named Ginger. Ginger is amazing—scientifically studied, tested, and certified a psychic medium through the Windbridge Research Center and the Forever Family Foundation, both of which are afterlife-study foundations.

She does a reading for me and brings in Julie and my father. I'm crying my eyes out during the reading and ask Ginger if she could train me, but she tells me she currently isn't training mediums. However, she refers me to someone named Michele, who she feels is really good and could help train me. Keep Ginger in mind—we'll come back to her later.

Before committing to training with Michele, I wanted to see how good she was, so I scheduled a reading with her. Michele, like Ginger, is a certified psychic medium, and she turned out to be just as amazing as Ginger had said. After the reading, I asked Michele if she would be willing to train me, and she agreed.

A few weeks later, before the training officially started, Michele conducted a psychic-medium assessment on me. Right in the middle of the assessment, Julie came through. Michele remarked that this was unusual, as it doesn't typically happen during assessments. She told me that Julie was going to help me with this journey, which didn't surprise me and brought me comfort.

Then Michele told me that I would be doing readings for people. In my mind, I thought, *Oh no, I'm not*, still struggling to fully believe that I'm a psychic medium. Julie, through Michele, reassured me to just allow it to happen and that she would be there to help me.

Michele trained me from early January 2024 to early April 2024, and we still stay in contact today. She quickly realized that I'm clairaudient (able to hear), clairvoyant (able to see), and clairsentient (able to sense) loved ones on the other side. This means that when I connect with a loved one in spirit, I can hear, see, and sense them. The prefix "clair" means clear, so "clairvoyant" means clear seeing, for example.

One thing I've managed to achieve by this point is the ability to clear my mind of all thoughts, just as Todd had previously advised me. I have to be honest—it wasn't easy. It took a lot of meditation, both with soft meditation music and in total silence.

Back to Michele and my training—honestly, I have to give all the credit to Michele for developing my psychic and medium abilities. Michele was trained by some of the best certified psychic mediums, including one who is internationally known and has appeared on TV. Like me, Michele saw ghosts and spirits as a young child.

I'll admit I wasn't the easiest student at first. My background as a US Army soldier, combined with how I was raised and educated, made it difficult for me to believe in psychic mediums. To say Michele was super kind, super patient, and super caring with me would be an understatement.

Imagine being told you were a psychic medium when you had never believed in that sort of thing your entire life until your wife transitioned. I tell people now that if, a year ago, someone had told me I'd be elected president of the USA, play for the Boston Red Sox, or become a psychic medium in less than a year, I would have ranked being a psychic medium as the least likely to happen.

Michele taught her students in both one-on-one and group sessions; we also had the option to practice more in voluntary psychic practice circles, in which we could hone our psychic and medium abilities as a group. I participated in both.

I don't recall exactly when, but during one of my early one-on-one sessions with Michele, I still had a lot of doubt. I kept telling her, "I don't believe I'm a medium."

She consistently replied, "Yes, you are, Alex."

I responded, "I don't think so."

She firmly, but kindly, insisted, "Yes, you are—you need to believe in yourself." It reached the point that she said to me in a very firm yet loving way, "Alex, I want you to repeat to yourself, both out loud and in your mind, 'I'm a medium; I'm a medium; I'm a medium.'" I told Michele I'd try to do that.

In another early one-on-one session, I told Michele I didn't understand the process of making a good connection with a loved one's spirit on the other side.

Once again, Michele was incredibly patient with me. She asked, "What do you not understand?"

I explained that I understood everything except the order of the steps to follow. She asked what I meant, and I told her that, in the Army, I was used to following steps—step one, do this; step two, do that, and so on.

She said, "Okay, get a piece of paper out, and write these steps down."

So I did. To this day, I still refer to those steps she gave me.

Around this time, something else strange happened. One night, I was sitting at home with Beeps, the cat. I had just finished talking to Julie out loud and was crying afterward. I was sitting on the couch with Beeps beside me when my cell phone rang. The caller ID showed "Private Number," which I don't normally answer because I assume it's a spam call. But for some reason, I answered this one.

It was a lady who said she was a Catholic nun. Right from the start, she seemed a bit bossy and very direct. She said, "Alex"—I still don't know how she knew my name—"how do you pray?"

I said, "Sister, I don't understand your question. What do you mean, 'how do I pray?'"

She then asked me to show her how I pray.

I said, "Okay," and started reciting the Our Father.

She interrupted me and said, "You're not praying."

I replied, kind of laughing at this point, "What do you mean, I'm not praying? Yes, I am."

She told me that I pray as if I were going to the grocery store to pick up milk, eggs, and bread—meaning I was just reciting something and not truly praying. She instructed me to pray as if I was actually talking to God and believed He was listening.

I promised I would. To this day, I still don't know who that Catholic nun was or where she was calling from.

At this point, I thought to myself, *I have the Bible, of course, but maybe I should look for some books on how to pray to God.* So I went to Walmart and a few other stores and bought several books on praying to God and Jesus. One book I particularly liked was called *Power of Prayer*.

Then it hit me—my friend Josh, who is a major in the Air Force, is someone I should reach out to. Josh is incredibly religious; he reads the Bible and prays all the time. I had known this about Josh for a number of years, even before Julie went to heaven.

I decided to give Josh a call and ask him for tips on how to pray. When I called, Josh told me he was currently traveling back home from Kirtland Air Force Base but would be happy to talk to me and share what he does when praying once he got back home. Funny side note: when I called Josh, he happened to be in an airport bathroom and apologized for all the flushing sounds in the background. But that's just Josh—a very religious, kind, and wonderful person.

Here's when another strange thing happened. As I mentioned before, it often felt as if someone was guiding me along the way. Later that day, Josh texted me: *I just landed in Charlotte and was sitting next to a pastor on the last flight. He and I spoke about prayer and praying. He said he's going to text me some things later on. I thought that was a little more than coincidence. Just thought I'd pass that along.*

I responded back to Josh: *Wow. That's amazing. Not a coincidence. Thanks, Josh.*

Back to Michele and training—I attended my first psychic practice circle via Zoom and finally got to see the other students Michele was training. There were about eight of us in the class, including me. Michele started by teaching us some tips on connecting with a loved one and then asked if anyone wanted to try and see what they could pick up from a loved one of another student. I volunteered, though I reminded her that I was new to this.

I shared that I was getting a man, provided his name, and described what he did for a living. Immediately, another student recognized whom I was talking about. Michele then encouraged me to go deeper and provide more information, which I did. I was kind of surprised by how accurate it seemed.

After the session, I texted Michele to ask her how I did. I also apologized for the crying, explaining that when I connect with someone's loved one on the other side, I can feel the overwhelming love they have for the person here. It can be challenging to speak when you're overcome with that emotion. Michele reassured me, saying I did great.

Before Julie went to heaven, I wasn't one to cry much, but now, connecting with spirits and feeling their deep love can bring me to tears.

As I trained with Michele, I also continued the healing sessions with Sharon and Lynne. On one particular visit to the Harmonic Egg, my sister Carol was visiting and decided to come along. While she waited in the reception area, I went in for my session with Lynne.

We talked about everything that was happening in my life, and Lynne reiterated what Michele had been telling me—I would eventually be reading for people. I hesitated and said I was only comfortable doing readings for family. Lynne laughed and assured me that I'd be reading for total strangers too. I couldn't see that happening, but she was confident.

Lynne, being the kind soul she is, gifted me some tools to help me along my journey: a set of angel tarot cards, a box of prayer cards, and a set of Story Cubes. Story Cubes are these little dice with symbols on each side; they can be used to tell stories or provide insight.

Lynne demonstrated how to use the Story Cubes, shaking them in her hand and tossing them onto the table, then interpreting what the symbols meant in relation to my life. Her reading was spot-on. She encouraged me to try it at home with my sister Carol. I was reluctant, feeling unsure about my abilities, but Lynne laughed and insisted that I could do it.

So when we got home, I took a deep breath and decided to give it a try. I shook the Story Cubes, tossed them onto the table, and began to tell my sister what I was picking up about her life. To my surprise, she confirmed that my reading was accurate. It was a strange but rewarding experience.

During one of our conversations, Lynne mentioned her friend Denise, who offered Reiki training. I was curious, especially since I was now fully immersed in learning about things that had never crossed my mind before Julie transitioned. Julie had always been the more spiritual one, and I'm sure she had known about these things, but she never forced them on me, knowing I wouldn't have listened back then.

For those who might not be familiar, Reiki is a form of energy healing that originated in Japan in 1922. It was first discovered by Mikao Usui during a period of intense meditation. Although the exact story of how he discovered Reiki is somewhat uncertain, what we do know is that he used his knowledge to teach others about the healing power of this energy-based practice.

Reiki comes from two words: "rei," meaning spiritual wisdom, and "ki," meaning life energy. Combined, these two words represent how Reiki works. Spiritual guidance enables the healer to use the universal life energy (ki) to promote spiritual, emotional, and physical healing. I found this interesting: the *Washington Post* reported in 2014 that in response to customer demand, at least sixty hospitals in the United States offered Reiki.

During a healing session, Reiki energy flows through the Reiki practitioner and into the person receiving the treatment. The healer can direct the energy, but it will go where it is most needed. Reiki healing is an incredibly powerful experience that touches a person's body, mind, and soul.

I called Denise and signed up for Reiki lessons; she is a Reiki master and shaman. Denise is wonderful and a great teacher who definitely takes it very seriously. There were times while she was teaching me when I thought it was as if I were in a hard college class.

As part of Reiki training, you learn about chakras. The word "chakra" means disk or wheel, and it refers to the energy centers in your body. Each of these wheels or disks of spinning energy corresponds to certain nerve bundles and major organs. To function at their best, your chakras need to stay open, or balanced. If they get blocked, you may experience physical or emotional symptoms related to the particular affected chakra. There are seven main chakras that run along your spine. They start at the root, or base, of your spine and extend to the crown of your head.

Crown Chakra
Third Eye Chakra
Throat Chakra
Heart Chakra
Solar Plexus Chakra
Sacral Chakra
Root Chakra

As part of the training and certification process, one of your key tasks is to scan a person with your hands, to identify areas of pain or problems in their body, and then to provide healing to those areas.

I vividly remember the day Denise brought in a lady for me to practice on. She looked very fit and healthy, so I was initially skeptical, wondering what could possibly be wrong with her. However, I trusted the process and applied what Denise had taught me. As I scanned her body with my hands, I was surprised to feel a distinct difference in energy in certain areas, which indicated where healing was needed. It was a remarkable experience, one that reinforced the idea that there is much more to healing than what we can see on the surface.

I completed the training and became Reiki I and II certified under Denise's guidance. This experience was a significant milestone in my journey, further opening my mind to the possibilities of energy healing and the unseen forces that guide us.

Reiki training is also known to help with psychic and medium abilities. Opening and aligning the chakras through Reiki can enhance a medium's ability to receive clear and accurate spiritual messages.

Personally, I found that Reiki not only helped me physically with my back pain from my time in the Army, but also emotionally and spiritually. It noticeably increased my mediumship abilities. Before Julie transitioned, I would have never even considered seeing someone for Reiki healing, but now I make it a point to do so at least once a month.

I'm continuing my training with Michele to become a proficient psychic medium. I'm starting to gain more confidence in doing readings for strangers, but I still struggle with the challenge of crying when I connect with the spirit of a loved one every time I do a reading as part of my training—not out of sadness, but because I can feel the profound love between the person and their loved one. It seems that not all mediums feel it as intensely as I do, or they've learned how to manage it, which is something I'm still working on.

Michele, as part of her training, has me read for people she brings into our Zoom sessions. In one of our psychic practice circle sessions, Michele showed us pictures on Zoom, and I seemed to pick up information quite well from the images. This led me to explore whether there are places online I could practice reading pictures for people who have lost a loved one.

I eventually found a forum in which I could offer picture readings, which I still prefer over in-person, Zoom, or phone readings—mainly because it helps me manage the emotional intensity. However, I do continue to do readings in all formats and offer healing sessions when people reach out to me.

Each step in this journey, from Reiki to psychic mediumship, has been transformative, helping me connect more deeply with the spiritual realm and offering comfort and healing to others, even as I continue to learn and grow.

In one particular case, an Army friend of mine—who, like me a year ago, was very skeptical about anything related to psychic abilities—reached out to me for help. His wife had a friend who had just given birth to a newborn baby girl with a very serious heart condition. The baby had been taken to a major state hospital for treatment, and the situation was critical.

Understanding the gravity of the situation, I asked my friend for the baby's name, explaining that I would push angelic healing to her during my prayers and meditation. He responded with a simple thank-you.

Though my friend shared my old skepticism, his willingness to reach out to me in such a dire moment showed how much he hoped for some kind of intervention. As I prayed and meditated, focusing on sending healing energy to the baby, I felt a deep sense of connection and purpose, hoping to bring some relief or healing to the child.

I kept asking the angels to please heal the little girl, praying with all my heart for her recovery. A few days later, I felt a sense of relief, as though she was improving. Trusting my intuition, I reached out to my friend and asked how the baby was doing.

He responded, "She's doing better. She just had her feeding tube out yesterday, and she is gaining weight."

I told my friend, "As you probably suspect, I already knew. An angel healer showed me her healing her heart and the veins running to her heart."

A couple of days later, he texted me: *I meant to text you yesterday morning—my wife told me the baby girl came home from the hospital.*

I want to be clear: I am not the one doing the healing; it's the angels. All I can do is ask them to please help heal someone. The power of their intervention is beyond anything I could achieve on my own. I'm just a conduit, sending out requests for their divine assistance.

By this point, I've fully accepted that I'm a psychic medium with some healing abilities that can help others. After completing my training with Michele, I realized just how much she had done for me. If you're reading this, Michele, thank you deeply for your teaching, kindness, compassion, and love—not only for guiding me through this journey, but also for helping me through such a challenging time in my life.

Now, I'm looking to continue my training, and to my surprise, Ginger is offering an advanced-mediumship class that could lead to certification as a psychic medium. I contacted Ginger, and she accepted me into the program, but she mentioned that she would need to assess my abilities by having me connect with and read a few of her loved ones on the other side.

Ginger, much like Michele, is kind, compassionate, patient, and loving. I'm incredibly blessed to have met both of them. I love them both like my own sisters, along with Sharon and Lynne. During my assessment, I was able to connect with Ginger's father and brother on the other side and provide her with evidential messages that confirmed the connection.

As of August 10, 2024, I'm still in training with Ginger and continue to do readings on the forum where people post pictures requesting a reading. This journey has been extraordinary, and I'm grateful for the guidance and support I've received from many loving people along the way.

CHAPTER 11
My Psychic-Mediumship Readings

I still miss Julie tremendously and talk to her daily, both out loud and in my mind. The tears still come because I miss her physical presence with me, but I've come to accept that she's okay on the other side, in heaven. I've found some peace in knowing that, one day, I'll be with her again, but I understand now that I need to complete my journey here on Earth before I can join her.

I believe that my calling to do readings for others stems from my deep understanding of the grief and pain people experience when a loved one transitions to the other side.

Through my own journey, I've come to realize that we don't truly die; instead, we transition to another existence where our loved ones who have gone before us are waiting to reunite. This belief has brought me comfort and purpose, and I hope to share that with others who are going through their own journeys of loss and healing.

Mediumship readings can be a unique and varied experience, both for the medium and for the person receiving the reading. When I connect with someone's loved one on the other side, the strength of that connection can differ—it's like having a one-bar or a five-bar signal on your cell phone. A strong connection allows the information to flow clearly, as if you were having a full conversation, while a weaker connection might only allow for whispers, single words, or images to come through.

In my experience, when I first connect with a spirit, I typically feel a physical sensation in my body, often warm chills. Following that, I might start receiving sentences, words, or images. These messages come to me in different ways—sometimes I feel them, sometimes I hear them, and sometimes I see them. It's not quite the same as having a conversation with someone on this side of life; the communication is more nuanced and can vary in clarity.

This understanding has helped me navigate the readings I do, and I try to convey to the people for whom I am reading that each session is unique. The messages might come through in different forms, but they all carry meaning and importance from their loved ones on the other side.

I completely understand why people might be skeptical about the idea of mediums connecting with loved ones on the other side. A year ago, I was in the same boat—I didn't believe it was possible. But now, after everything I've experienced, I do believe it is real. What I'm sharing here includes some of the readings I've done, in hopes that it might help you decide for yourself whether or not it's possible. I genuinely believe my wife, Julie, is helping me with these readings.

One of the things I appreciate about the particular on-line forum I use for readings is the anonymity it provides. People use usernames, like "redbird9932," rather than their real names, so as a medium, you have no idea who they are, where they're from, or anything else about them. This setup ensures that the readings are as unbiased and genuine as possible.

For those who might be wondering, I've never charged for a reading. All the readings I do are free. I have been offered money, but I always decline. Instead, I suggest that if they want to give back, they could help someone in need—maybe buy food and water for a homeless person, donate to a shelter, or contribute to a food bank. But I leave that decision up to them. My focus is on providing healing, both for the person receiving the reading and for their loved ones on the other side who want to send messages.

I also make it clear to everyone that I'm new to this. It's been less than a year since I started doing readings. Despite that, I've already completed over 400 readings. My username on the forum is "Tasty-Marketing-2286," a name I chose because it's so far removed from my background as a retired US Army officer that no one could possibly identify me. But I guess people will know now.

MY READINGS
BASED ON PICTURES ALONE

Anything from them? :(

· 8h

I'm new at this. Are they your parents? I'm getting you are their daughter? Did your mom pass before your dad? She is smiling and said she was there to meet him? Not sure why I'm getting Louisiana? Do you have a couple of daughters? Does the name Anna mean anything? Your father comes forward to me much stronger than your mom—he is saying he is very proud of young and could not have asked for a better daughter. He said I know I was a little hard on you at times but only wanted the best for you. They both love you very much. I can feel their love radiating through me--very beautiful people and souls. Not sure why he shows me them like camping on the other side and walking around in nature--they are both smiling and saying she will understand. I'm starting to cry from their love so will lose the connection with them--I'm sorry. They both love you so very much and do visit you and your children. Hope some of this has meaning to you. Many Blessings.

You were so spot on. Yes, they're my parents. I do live in Louisiana. My mom did pass first. I do have two kids and my parents always loved taking us camping as kids. You have an amazing gift. I haven't stopped smiling and crying since reading your comment. Thank you beyond words. 💜💜

What does she have to say?

Reading Request

Please & thank you in advance 🖤📷

New at this. Is she your mother? Did she pass after a long illness--not sure why I'm feeling chest/headache. I heard the month of Feb. She said "You worry too much and yes I'm fine--she is smiling." Boy was he surprised to see me when he came to this side--she said you would know what that means. I heard Honey I'm fine. Could she be playful sassy at times? Music and pictures? This one is nice, don't you think--she is showing me clothes? I've got to get my hair fixed. Did she like going out to eat and sweet tea? She love jeans also--I know some of this you can see in the picture but it's what she is telling me. Texas--do you live in Texas. Cornbread and you have to make it like this. Yes, I'm still around you and visit you. I love that girl so much and she knows it, we were mom and daughter but best friends also? Love you back? Hope some of this has meaning to you. Many Blessings.

⋮　　↩ Reply　🔖　⬆ 1 ⬇

Wow, thank you! I'm fighting back tears here. Happy to provide feedback via DM 🖤

Help please!

Reading Request

I need an emergency session with my mom, can anyone help me? Please! It's urgent!

New at this. Did your mom pass recently after a long battle with cancer. I'm feeling something in my chest and breast area. Your mom said Not to worry about her she is always around you and your little boy. Something about you will make the right decision about something--just relax? Your mom is a very kind and loving women, and smart. Do you have a ring of hers. She said sometimes when you hold the ring you can feel her prescence. Not sure why I got the letter K? Is there a Sharon? She said sometimes you think she is not still around you but she said she is. Please don't be sad and cry--she said she hears you when you talk to her outside? Hope some of this has meaning to you. Many Blessings

Omg Tasty... you are new but that touched me. I have goose bumps. Oh my god ur so kind :) My parents are gone and I'm facing such horrible horrible circumstances and I need help. Would u also be able to help me. I'm just trying everything. Please if u can if not I totally 🙏 appreciate that not to worry. Thank uou

146

Does my dad have any messages for me?

`Reading Request`

• 3h

New at this. Your parents were not from the USA? I'm seeing a warm tropical area? Your father is saying yes he is around you allot. He's seems a little worried about someone--maybe your mother? He said do wants makes you happy and wait for the right guy? He said you will know when you meet the right guy and you will? He said you were a very good girl growing up and he is proud of you. He said "Hey please don't go walking around the city at night? Not sure why I heard Rosa--not sure if name or flower? She is my baby please let her know how much I love her? he said you are a smart girl and will make the right decisions? Hope some of this has meaning to you. Many Blessings

⋮   ↩ Reply   ⚬   ⬆ 2 ⬇

Wow I'm speechless 😭 You hit the nail in the head on every point. I can't thank you enough. Do you offer reading sessions? If so, I would love to connect please!!

⋮   ↩   ⚬   ⬆ 1 ⬇

Anything?

Would be greatly appreciated

• 2h ago

New at this. Is she your mother? I'm getting Carribean area? Did she speak Spanish? Not sure why New York came up? I heard the word Popi also? She said and she is speaking a little fast for me "Yes, yes, please finish school." She siad "You are such a smart girl". Not sure why I heard Rosa/Rosalita? She is showing me her in the kitchen and she is stirring a big pot and asking me if it smells good" It smells great whatever she is cooking. I love this lady, lots of joy and kindness in her soul. She loves you so, so much, she is kissing her hands by her face and blowing the kiss to you. Hope this has some meaning. Many Blessings.

⊖ ⬆ 1 ⬇   ⬜ Reply   ⋯

omg. you are amazing. she is dominican and yes speaks spanish. thank you so much. i am willing to pay if there's anything else - try to relay any message to her sons (she is my MIL) thank you 😭 😭 💜💜💜💜💜

Is there anything you can feel about her? Is she still around at all?

`Reading Request`

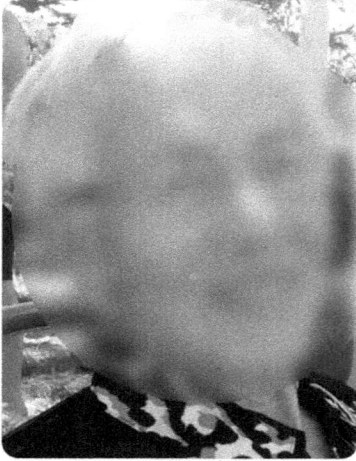

I miss her dearly and wish I had spent more time with her before she passed, so bad.

⬆ 14 ⬇ 💬 2   ↪

⚫ Reply Redacted 2000 · 11h

New to this. I'm getting she is your grandmother. I'm seeing like a breathing tube before she passed but of course she is perfectly fine now. She shows me herself walking around outside in nature and looking at birds. She said "Of course I'm around and visit you". Does Canada mean anything. Something with teaching or teacher. Not sure why I'm hearing something about your father -- like she is worried about him. I heard her say "Come take a look at this, she is trying to show me something she made?" I heard the word grace also. She loves you and doesn't want you to be sad, she said enjoy your life, I'm around and visit. Hope this has some meaning to you? Many Blessings.

⋮   ↩ Reply   ⬆ 3 ⬇

Thank you for this... it took my breath away. Would you be okay with it if I private message you and ask some questions?

Any messages? He's been on my mind lately

⚫ Reply Redacted · 13h

New at this. Are you his daughter? I'm hearing like a Middle Eastern Accent, maybe Egypt? Not sure why I'm hearing the word Kali? I'm not familiar with the Middle East or Egypt. I'm feeling he was good with money. Something with food and restaurants. He is telling me "She is a very smart girl and love her very much" and "Yes, I am proud of you". I'm seeing a dance celebration of some sort that is cultural in nature. He is now saying "Take care of your family and the little ones, I am happy and healthy now. He sends you much love.

⋮   ↩ Reply   ⬆ 1 ⬇

Wow this seems spot on. I appreciate this more than you know.

⋮   ↩   ⬆ 2 ⬇

I just want to make sure my nana wasn't scared or suffering when she passed alone. She passed in the ICU on April 12th in the evening and the hospital didn't inform us until we called to check in the next day. Anything would help, thank you!

New at this. Your nana was not scared or suffering when she transitioned. She said there were people waiting for her on the other side--I see two men and a lady--could be husband and her parents. Is someone in the military or was in the military? Do you have a brother. She said don't feel bad you had to take care of that little guy? Do you have a son? I heard the name Deborah/ Debbie and Susan. Something with dancing/swirling around. Hope some of this has meaning to you. Many Blessings

Reply 5

This is all pretty spot on!! I would not have known you were new to this.

You don't have to answer this, but can I ask you how she seemed to you? I hope she's happy and free. She had a stroke about 12 years ago and was never the same.

Thank you so much for taking the time to give me some peace. I appreciate you

Does this man come through for anyone? He was very close to me.

Reading Request

• 4h ago

New at this. Not sure why I was getting flying. Almost like flying a helicopter or rode in one. Is he your father? I know it's obvious but he had a great sense of humor and loved children and pets. I'm getting something with Canada? Was he a fireman at one time? Not sure if you know someone named Jim? I'm seeing a pair of boots also. Do you have a brother? He is saying he loves you and does come visit with his babies--he's talking about some of the small dogs with him on the other side.

3 Reply ···

This makes complete sense, oh my goodness thank you so much

Can anyone do a reading for me please, lost my uncle so suddenly and too soon. Anything is really appreciated <3. Thank you so much in advance.

Reading Request

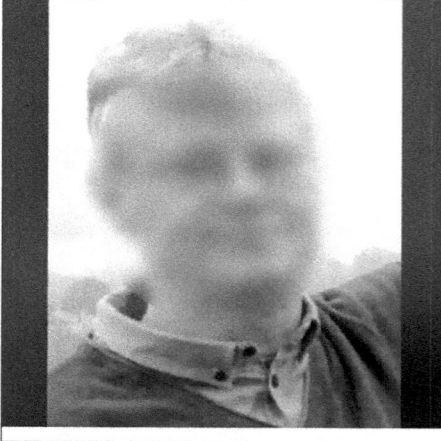

New at this. Are you and him from UK/England? I feel he passed with something related to his heart? I'm seeing cricket and soccer. Something about Manchester United? I don't know anything about soccer or cricket so assuming that's a team. He said "Mate get on with yourself already I'm perfectly fine" and "It's wonderful that you think of me but I'm good here and visit you". He said "Now don't worry yourself and go have a cup pf tea or in the evening have a drink for me? -- he's laughing when he said that. I heard the name Carl also?? He said now tell everyone I love them but I'm fine and with some family and friends on the other side. Hope this has some meaning to you? Many Blessings.

2 Reply

Absolutely, this was incredibly accurate. Honestly thank you so so much for doing this. I really appreciate it. My name is Calum and he called me Cal for short, Manchester United is my football team. He passed so suddenly and my mum was really affected by it. Showing her this will bring such a big smile on her face so thank you.

---

does anyone get anything from her? my grandmother (nene)

New at this. Did your grandmother pass with something related to the chest--coughing? Your nene is a very loving and kind person--I feel she loved people and animals. Not sure why I heard the word Turkey? Is she Turkish? She is showing me her drinking a tea from a small decorative flower cup and smiling. Now I'm seeing an island with a beautiful coastline? She is laughing and saying pets love you like they love her--something you got from her." I see her with some animals on the other side and she loves being with them. She said she needs to fix her hair and laughing--I told her it looked fine. Something about a bracelet and necklace?--she said oh so beautiful. She loves you and said she comes around -- was there a recent event--she said she was there. Hope this has some meaning to you. Many Blessings.

1 Reply

Oh my god YES TO ALL OF THIS!!!! She was from Cyprus (so yes, very very Turkish!), but lived majority of her time on a small island in Turkey called Çanakkale- her home was right on the coast. She passed away from something heart related, and my mom (her daughter) just had to have live-saving open heart surgery and I have been saying it probably was the same thing that Nene had. I did just find out I'm pregnant, and it's been decided if it's a girl we are giving the baby her name to honor her. Such a strong, strong woman. 💜

Reading Request

I'm new at this. It's obvious you are from Canada and a french speaking part of Canada. Your father was very kind and friendly. I feel he worked a job that had something to do with helping people. Is your mother on the other side--I see a lady next to him. He was very smart and understood business matters. I'm seeing him with a calculator. He tried to live healthly and eat healthy but this illness snuck up on him out of the blue. I'm not sure why I'm hearing a french name that starts with E like Eric and a girls name that starts with A. He said you are a wonderful daughter and always had his humor and positive outlook on things. He wants me to tell you thank you. Do you have something of his like a watch or ring. He said children's laughter makes him happy, along with your beautiful smile. Such a kind and loving person. He said he wants you to be happy and not sad. He also said he is not gone just on the other side. He is holding up a glass of what looks like red wine and smiling. He loves you and your children very much and does visit. Hope some of this has meaning to you. Many Blessings

He is probably with his dear sister on the other side... That is shockingly so right what you tell me here! It made me cry 😿. I have his ring with me 💜 Your message lights up my day. Thank you soooo much

⋮ ↰ ⟳ ⬆ 3 ⬇

151

CHAPTER 12

We Don't Die—Closing Message

I t's become clear to me that death isn't the end. We don't die; we transition to the other side—whether you call it another realm, paradise, heaven, or whatever feels right to you. Julie is in heaven now.

Julie didn't die, and I'm certain that one day, when it's my time, I'll be with her again. Does Julie visit me? Absolutely. Does she know I love her, and do I know she loves me? Without a doubt. Love doesn't die either. This truth isn't just about Julie and me—it applies to anyone who has lost a loved one.

Here's a recap of the supporting evidence that has convinced me, beyond a reasonable doubt, that we don't die but instead transition to the other side/heaven.

Belief in God and the Afterlife: About 85 percent of the world's population, which equates to approximately seven billion people, believe in God and some form of afterlife. This widespread belief suggests a collective understanding of something beyond this life.

Signs from the Other Side: The angel wings and other signs I've received from the other side, including those from Julie, cannot be easily explained by anything in our physical world. These experiences point to a continued existence beyond death.

Reincarnation Studies by UVA: The University of Virginia's Division of Perceptual Studies, founded by Dr. Ian Stevenson, continues to validate the phenomenon of reincarnation, providing evidence that our spirit persists across lifetimes.

Life-between-Lives Research by Dr. Newton: The work of Dr. Michael Newton and his institute has provided insights into our spiritual existence and the purpose of our earthly lives through past-life regression studies.

Near-Death Experiences (NDEs): Research by Dr. Bruce Greyson and others has shown that people who have had NDEs often report experiences of the afterlife, including awareness of events around them while unconscious. My own experience during Ketamine treatment, which is similar to an NDE, further confirms the existence of an afterlife.

Institute of Noetic Sciences (IONS): This organization, founded by Apollo 14 astronaut Dr. Edgar Mitchell, is composed of highly accredited scientists who explore common but often misunderstood phenomena, including consciousness and life after death.

CIA's Gateway Process: Developed by the Monroe Institute in the 1970s, this process uses meditation-like techniques combined with sound technology to induce altered states of consciousness, allowing for healing, spiritual growth, and access to new information across space and time.

The Monroe Institute: For over fifty years, the Monroe Institute has been a leading center for exploring and experiencing expanded states of consciousness. The only prerequisite for attending their classes and training is an open mind and the understanding that our existence extends beyond the physical realm.

Work of Thomas Edison and Nikola Tesla: Both Edison and Tesla, two of the most brilliant minds of our time, worked on devices intended to communicate with spirits on the other side. Their belief in the possibility of connecting with spirits suggests that they acknowledged our transition to another realm after death.

Electronic Voice Phenomenon (EVP): My own experiences with EVP, receiving clear messages from Julie, reinforce the idea that communication with the other side is possible.

Experiences with Accredited Psychic Mediums: The psychic mediums I've worked with provided me with evidential information that could only have come from Julie, demonstrating their ability to communicate with spirits.

My Experience as a New Psychic Medium: My journey as a new psychic medium, as shared in the last chapter, has provided me with direct experiences that confirm the existence of life beyond this physical realm.

First and foremost, God wants us to love each other and not cause harm. We are all a part of God, much like your children are a part of you. As spiritual beings, we each carry a piece of God within us. Just as a parent doesn't want their children to hurt one another, God, as our divine parent, doesn't want us to inflict pain on each other. Though I don't fully understand how God can feel every one of us, and the harm we inflict on one another, He *does* feel that pain.

I'll be the first to admit that I didn't say, "I love you," enough to the people in my life, and for that, I'm deeply sorry. Today, I make it a point to love everyone, because I now realize we are all connected in some profound way. I'm not sure why it's often difficult for people to say, "I love you." Maybe it's out of fear of being hurt, but I've learned that the pain of not expressing love is far greater.

We are all spirits sharing a human experience on this place we call Earth. One day, we will all return as spirits to the other side, which I call heaven. On the other side, there is love, compassion, and friendship. So why can't we have that here?

Imagine—as I know you can because I'm speaking to the spirit within you—what it would be like if we all stopped hating each other and instead chose to love one another. Wars would cease, hunger would disappear, sadness and pain would fade, violence would vanish, and killings would end—all across the world. When you consider that from your spiritual perspective, you have to ask, "How did we get to the world we live in today?" The answer is simple: we stopped loving each other.

Let me emphasize this one more time—God does not want us to hurt each other. He told me this, and He feels all of us and all of our pain. I believe it's time we stop making God feel that pain. One of my new favorite sayings is "If you can hate me for no reason, why can't I love you for no reason?"

I still miss Julie and love her more with each passing day. I thank God for sending her into my life for thirty-nine years. I know that one day I will be with her on the other side, just as you will be with your loved ones. We don't die—we transition to be with our loved ones on the other side. There is an illusion of separation, but the veil between the two worlds is thin. Your loved ones are still around, and you will be with them when it's your time.

Many Blessings and Much Love to You.

JOURNEY ON ANGEL WINGS

The true story of looking for answers after a loved one transitions to heaven. Many of the things he saw and discovered, due to his background and upbringing, were not possible in his mind.

What he didn't know, you most likely don't know either. This book will make you cry, laugh, discover things you don't know, help heal your grief, and open your eyes to the truth about who we all are.

This book is dedicated to my wife, Julie, whom I love more than words can describe. She is an angel who helped me after she went to heaven. She is still with me, just as your loved ones on the other side are still with you. I didn't believe that before. Now, I'm 1,000-percent convinced it is true.

www.ingramcontent.com/pod-product-compliance
Lightning Source LLC
Chambersburg PA
CBHW070836100426
42813CB00003B/644